do
angels
really
have
wings?

do
angels
really
have
wings?

and 199 Other Questions
about God, Life, and the Bible

with

Don Cole, Mike Kellogg, Michael Rydelnik,
Rosalie de Rosset, Winfred Neely,
and other writers from
Today in the Word

MOODY PUBLISHERS

CHICAGO

Edited by Kevin Mungons, Pamela J. Pugh, Heather Moffitt, and Elena After
Interior and cover design: Erik M. Peterson
Cover illustration of frowning emoji copyright © 2017 by calvindexter/iStock (639295374). All rights reserved. Cover illustration of wings copyright © 2017 by nadia_bormotova/iStock (656172012). All rights reserved. Cover illustration of clouds copyright © 2017 by tupungato/iStock (862712432). All rights reserved.

ISBN: 978-0-8024-1858-6

We hope you enjoy this book from Moody Publishers. Our goal is to provide high-quality, thought-provoking books and products that connect truth to your real needs and challenges. For more information on other books and products written and produced from a biblical perspective, go to www.moodypublishers.com or write to:

Moody Publishers
820 N. LaSalle Boulevard
Chicago, IL 60610

1 3 5 7 9 10 8 6 4 2

Printed in the United States of America

Contents

INTRODUCTION:

Do Angels
Really Have Wings?

The question seems fair enough, something an average person would ask—not out of skepticism, but genuine curiosity.

It's okay to have questions. God even poses questions to us, provoking our thinking about the Christian life. When Jesus washed the feet of His disciples, He asked "Do you understand what I have done for you?" (John 13:12).

For thirty years, the devotional magazine *Today in the Word* has featured a popular Question-and-Answer column. A team of gifted writers draws on their years of practical experience to offer solid answers, clearly explaining what the Bible teaches.

And not just about angels. But every day we are confronted with difficult issues we can't figure out. The problem of pain and suffering, dealing with the past, handling conflicts at home and work and church. Or perhaps our friends bombard us with hot topics like politics, abortion, and suicide. Or perhaps you've got a question about a point of doctrine or responding to a current issue or you'd like to know what the Bible says about _____.

Does the Bible really have an answer to your questions? Yes! We hope you will pick this book up many times. We've designed it so you can jump in anywhere and find interesting questions and answers. And if you're looking for a specific topic or issue, the indexes at the back will point you toward pertinent selections. Perhaps you can also use this as a resource in your own teaching and Bible study ministry—the indexes at the back with help you find Scripture passages and topics.

And keep asking questions!

PART ONE

Did Jesus have grandparents?

and other questions about God, Jesus, and the Holy Spirit

1. Is God really a person?

Not in precisely the same way that we are persons. We are just human beings. Nevertheless, God has personality and is, in that sense, a person. At the burning bush, He told Moses, "I AM WHO I AM" (Ex. 3:14). God also told Moses to tell the people of Israel, "The LORD, the God of your fathers—the God of Abraham, the God of Isaac and the God of Jacob—has sent me to you. This is my name forever, the name you shall call me from generation to generation" (Ex. 3:15). *All* the names given to God in Scripture denote personality. Furthermore, the Bible uses personal pronouns with respect to God, as in John 17:3: "Now this is eternal life: that they know you, the only true God, and Jesus Christ, whom you have sent."

The Bible ascribes attributes of personality (or personhood) to God. God grieves (Gen. 6:6), He loves (Rev. 3:19), etc. Thus, the testimony of the Bible is that God is indeed a person.

—*D. C.*

2. What is the image of God in mankind? How do you get it, and can you lose it?

Every person is born with the image of God, and you cannot lose it. So what is this image of God?

The dictionary defines an image as "the reproduction or imitation of the form of a thing or a person." Mankind, as made in the image of God, is intended to resemble God, though not physically, of course. God is spirit, not material (John 4:24). Nobody has ever looked like God.

Genesis 1:26–31 and 2:7–25 reveal that God created man

in His own image, and that Eve was not an afterthought as she was also a creature made in God's image. The first stage of Adam's creation was shaping the man from clay. Second, God breathed into his nostrils the breath of life, and the clay came to life as a living being. The clay model did not become merely an intelligent animal; he became the bearer of the image of God.

This means that he resembled his Creator. The least that can be said about the Creator is that He is a person: He thinks, He feels, and He acts. In other words, He has intellect and emotion, and the ability to act in accordance with those properties. Theologians and other thinkers draw up lists of properties that define the image of God, including self-consciousness, self-transcendence, self-determination, the power of abstract thought, freedom of will (as contrasted with animal instinct), awareness of God and communion with Him, and the hope of eternal life.

The image of God was not lost when Adam sinned, but it was badly defaced. (See the following texts: Gen. 9:6; Acts 17:28; and James 3:9.) All of us are spiritually damaged. The only human being in history in whom the image of God was unblemished was Jesus. But, through the redemption that is in Him, the image of God is being restored to its pristine state in everyone who submits to Him in repentance and faith. The process begins with the new birth and continues until we reach our heavenly home (Rom. 8:29; 1 Cor. 15:49; 2 Cor. 3:18; Eph. 4:24).

—*D. C.*

3. A friend, based on Hebrews 2:18 and 4:15, says that Jesus could have sinned but did not. Is he right?

He is half-right: Jesus did not sin. The unanswered question, then, is could He have sinned? The answer is an emphatic no! He was impeccable, meaning that He was not able to sin. True, Hebrews 4:15 says He was "tempted in every way, just as we are," but in the Greek text, the words that follow, "yet he did not sin," lack a verb and should be translated, "apart from sin." Able not to sin, as some say, was not the case; He was not able to sin.

For those who insist that the words, "in every way," mean exactly that, and no less, consider 1 Corinthians 15:27: "Now when it says that 'everything' has been put under him, it is clear that this does not include God himself." Everything or every way does not always mean, "with no exception whatsoever."

The temptations that trouble us sinners most persistently depend on our sinful nature. Jesus did not have a sinful nature. He was incapable of any of the acts (or impulses) of the sinful nature listed in Galatians 5:19–21. Hebrews 6:18 says, "It is impossible for God to lie." Transfer that affirmation to Jesus, and we can conclude that it was impossible for Him to sin. That was the uniform testimony of three preeminent apostles—Peter, Paul, and John: "[Jesus] committed no sin" (1 Peter 2:22); "him who had no sin" (2 Cor. 5:21); and "in him is no sin" (1 John 3:5).

The value of Christ's death on our behalf depends on who He was. True, He embraced perfect humanity; He became a human being. He was like us, except that He did not have a sinful nature. He became human, but He did not cease to be the Son of God. As a perfect human being—if that were all He was—He could not have died vicariously for the sins of the world. He was the Lamb of God, to be sure—"without blemish or defect" (1 Peter 1:19)—but He was more than that. He was the Son of God, sinless and impeccable in all His parts.

—*D. C.*

4. Muslims admit that Jesus was a great prophet, but they say Muhammad, coming later, was greater. Which of the two was the greater?

You ask the wrong question. It might be possible to compare and contrast Muhammad with a prophet like Elijah or Amos. But it is impossible to compare him with Christ, because Christ was not a mere man. When, on the Mount of Transfiguration, Peter tried to put Moses and Elijah on the same level as Jesus, a cloud enveloped them and a terrifying voice spoke from the cloud, saying, "This is my Son, whom I love; with him I am well pleased. Listen to him!" (Matt. 17:5). Jesus is God's Son, not a mere prophet. But He also functioned as a prophet by being God's ultimate spokesman (see Heb. 1:1–4). He revealed the mind of the Father in all that He said and did. And then He made atonement for sin. Muhammad could never compare to the person or work of our Lord Jesus.

—*D. C.*

5. What does Matthew mean by the phrase, "blasphemy against the Spirit will not be forgiven" (Matt. 12:31)? Does this mean that there are some sins that cannot be forgiven? Can a believer ever commit this sin?

The discussion concerning the precise nature of this unforgivable sin is both extensive and controversial. Some in the early church thought that this sin was the denial of prophetic inspiration in general; others thought it was a form of post-conversion apostasy. Perhaps the most popular view is to equate the unforgivable sin with the rejection of the gospel. Those who refuse to embrace the forgiveness of sins offered through the cross have no other recourse for the atonement of their transgressions. In this interpretation, the unforgivable sin is the sin of unbelief, which John seems to affirm in 3:18 and 16:9 and also 1 John 5:16.

While this is a possible interpretation, it does not seem to fit within the context of Matthew 12. In this passage, the Pharisees have attributed the energizing force behind Jesus' miraculous healing to the prince of demons, Satan. They are not persuaded by the testimony and work of Jesus. They want to be a stumbling block to anyone else who might consider becoming a follower of Jesus Christ. Right after the miraculous healing, verse 23 says that all the people were astonished and wondered if Jesus was indeed the Son of David. At this point the Pharisees, in an attempt to dissuade them, say that Jesus is a pawn of Satan.

The "blasphemy against the Spirit" describes a heart that

is so hardened that it not only refuses to see the divine in the work of Christ, but it also actively prevents others from coming to Him. This interpretation fits the context. Those who oppose Jesus seek to scatter the Jews rather than gather them up into the kingdom of God (v. 30). Even in the presence of one of the great miracles in the Gospels—the healing of a demon-possessed, blind, and mute man—the hearts of the Pharisees were unmoved. These religious leaders had closed their hearts to any testimony of the Spirit that affirms Jesus as the Great One sent from God. This is the unforgivable sin.

Other passages within the Bible affirm this interpretation. Deuteronomy speaks of the worship of idols (which may persuade others to do so) as a sin that will not be forgiven (29:18–20). Those who have caused a little one to stumble would be better off with a millstone hung around their neck and thrown into the sea (Matt. 18:6). And the book of Hebrews speaks of those who have experienced the testimony of the Spirit to some degree and then rejected it; how can they be brought back to repentance (6:6)?

Finally, can a believer commit this sin? Personally, I do not believe an individual who has genuinely confessed Jesus as Lord can publicly oppose the work of God in the world by attributing it to something evil. Pastorally, anyone who fears having committed this sin should not worry; an apostate would not even consider worrying about having committed this sin.

—D. R.

6. A good friend says anger is okay, that it is even okay to be mad at God. Is he right?

Less than half right. Most of the Bible's references to anger are negative, and sometimes silly. Jonah was angry because God didn't destroy Nineveh. The prodigal son's brother was angry because their father celebrated the return of the prodigal. Jonah's anger would have been understandable if directed at, say, a conquering Israelite general. But he was angry at God, and to be angry at God is to be ridiculous as well as sinful. The older brother sounded like a petulant child; he made a fool of himself.

Anger need not always be sinful. Sometimes, as when a sex offender abuses a child, or when an elected official steals public funds, anger is appropriate. A ho-hum response to such crimes would be inexcusable. However, Paul warns us, "In your anger do not sin" (Eph. 4:26), and, "Get rid of all bitterness, rage and anger" (Eph. 4:31). We probably justify anger that is really intolerable. As James observes, "human anger does not produce the righteousness that God desires" (James 1:20).

Two additional considerations: first, more than one word in the original languages is rendered "anger." They are not entirely synonymous. Hence, a word study would be useful. Second, some of the writers of the Psalms were sorely distressed because of God's *apparent* indifference to their plight, and they may *seem* to us to have been angry. But they were never angry at God. After registering bewilderment in the face of social injustice and other anomalies, they ended their psalms with expressions of faith in God, and praise. They remembered that God is God. So should we.

—D. C.

7. If John's gospel did not use the term *Trinity*, why should we use the term? I just cannot understand: if there is but one God, how can He be made of three coequal persons working in unity? Doesn't one mean singular?

This is probably the most frequently asked and the most difficult question one can pose concerning the Christian faith. Yet it is so central to our faith that legions of theologians and philosophers have dared to tread these sacred grounds. Any response, especially in this limited format, will be incomplete and may be unsatisfying.

Let me begin by noting that while the term Trinity is not explicitly found in the Scriptures, the concept surely is. This doctrine is composed of three basic beliefs: (1) there is one God; (2) the Father is God; Jesus is God; and the Holy Spirit is God; and (3) all three divine persons are distinct.

As you have correctly noted, this presents the Christian with a dilemma. Either there is one God, and therefore, only one divine person; or, there are three divine persons, and therefore, three gods. But orthodox Christianity rejects both of these options as being heretical.

One route is to argue that there is one divine essence, which is constituted by three distinct persons, each identical to that divine essence. The oneness of the Trinity would refer to this divine essence. The threeness would refer to each of the divine persons, who simply are that one divine essence. This way of viewing things raises the issue of counting. How can there be only one essence when there are three divine persons identical to that one essence? That's like saying one equals three.

But one could argue that God transcends the human sphere in such a way that our concepts like "essence" or "person" cannot capture the rich details of the divine sphere. Think of it this way. A drawing by definition cannot be both a circle and a triangle. This is the case because one's perspective is that of a flat plane—two-dimensional. But if we expand our world into three dimensions, then we could have an object, such as a cone, which could be seen as a triangle from one perspective and a circle from a different perspective. It is the two-dimensional world's inability to capture the three-dimensional nature of the cone that produces this logical problem. Applying this to the issue at hand, our human concepts are like two-dimensional drawings trying to capture the reality of a three-dimensional divine Being.

The other route one can go is to argue that when we say there is one God, we mean that there is one "Godhead"—one divine society or family. In this case the Father, Son, and Spirit are members of the same divine family. The problem facing this particular model is whether the belief in one "Godhead" is as monotheistic as the belief in "one God." This understanding of the Trinity seems to position Christianity dangerously close to polytheism. But at the same time, its advantage is in its logical clarity. The oneness of the Trinity references the Godhead; the threeness references the Father, Son, and Spirit, who are members of that one divine family.

Different orthodox Christian theologians and philosophers support both of these interpretations. Those who desire to affirm a strong sense of monotheism tend to opt for the first model presented. Those who believe that conceptual precision is absolutely necessary in the formulation of our doctrines tend to opt for the second.

No matter where our disagreements may be concerning this most complex but crucial doctrine, we cannot forget that the triune nature of God is another way of saying what John has written in his first epistle: "God is love." From all of eternity, the Christian God is one whose essence is love, a selfless love of one person for another; a love so pure that it can only be pictured by the love of a parent for their only child.

—*D. R.*

8. I'm eleven years old, and I want to know why God made us if He knew that we would be sinners.

I'm eighty years old, and I often ponder the question. Many Bible students believe the answer follows three lines: First, God is love. Second, He seems to have wanted a bigger or better object of His love than angels. Third, He saw past Adam's sin and ruin to a new heaven and earth populated by redeemed people. The world to come would more than compensate for the sorrows of the first earth and its inhabitants.

"For God so loved the world," John 3:16 says, "that he gave his one and only Son." For reasons we do not fully fathom, God loved the work of His hands. Maybe that is why He created: He loved the world even before His act of creation.

Isaiah 43:7 gives an additional hint: "Everyone who is called by my name, whom I created for my glory." And in Isaiah 43:21 God says that He created His people for Himself, for a specific purpose: "that they may proclaim my praise."

It seems that God created us as an expression of His love and to receive our praise. Despite our sin, He has made a way for us to spend eternity with Him when the sin and sorrow of the past will be forgotten.

—*D. C.*

9. What year was Jesus born? According to Matthew, Jesus was born before Herod the Great died (4 BC, see Matt. 2:1–23) and according to Luke, He was born when Quirinius was governor of Syria, a position Quirinius took up around AD 6–7 (see Luke 2:2).

Matthew makes it clear that the Lord Jesus was born while Herod ruled. He died in 4 BC, so most Bible students surmise that the Lord Jesus was born a year or two earlier, sometime between 6 BC and early 4 BC. Matthew and Luke both place the birth of the Lord Jesus near the end of the reign of Herod. So the Lord Jesus was born sometime between 6 and 4 BC.

Josephus, the ancient Jewish historian, records that Quirinius became governor after the Romans removed Herod's son, Archelaus, as king in AD 6, and he carried out a census (or registration) of his entire domain early in his governorship (see Luke 2:1–3). On the surface this appears to contradict Matthew's account. A good explanation is to translate Luke 2:2 in a slightly different way. The key word is *proton*, translated "first," as in "This was the first census that took place while Quirinius was governor of Syria." When this word is used adverbially, it can mean "before." That's the way it was used in John 15:18, when the Lord Jesus said that the world "hated me first." Luke's point was that the Lord Jesus was born during a census, requiring Joseph and Mary to travel to their familial town; but this census is not to be confused with the more well-known census conducted ten years later by Quirinius. Luke's desire to be precise (see Luke 1:3–4) caused him to differentiate the census at the birth of Jesus from the later one.

—*M. R.*

10. I am wondering if God (as distinct from Christ) has emotions. I have heard some pastors and theologians claim that God has no emotions. It is very hard for me to think about or feel close to a kind of robot God.

Some time ago, a number of theologians did articulate a doctrine known as the "impassability of God" in which they contended that God was without what they called "passions." One could suggest that this stems from a fear that God would be seen as unstable because He had emotions. I myself have heard this teaching in classrooms. Such an image of God as what philosophers call an "unmoved mover" with little connection to us as human beings is more a product of Greek philosophy's emphasis on the dualism between flesh and spirit than on biblical teaching. Such a God becomes remote, the proverbial white-bearded "man in the sky" looking at us indifferently from the heavenly balcony.

I heard a fine sermon by Erwin Lutzer, pastor of The Moody Church, on this subject and was heartened again to hear that the answer was yes, God does have emotions; the evidence for this is in Scripture. First of all, it is important to note that God's emotions are not identical to ours; God is not subject to the dark side of emotions or to instability. As John Calvin said, God "lisps" to us in language we can understand. So the Bible tells us that He loves (John 3:16), He is grieved (Gen. 6:6), He becomes angry (Deut. 1:37), He is filled with pity (Judg. 2:18), He has compassion (Ps. 103:13), and He rejoices over us (Isa. 62:5), to name only a few. In the words of the old hymn, "The love of God is greater far / than tongue or pen can ever tell; It goes beyond the highest star / and reaches to the lowest hell. . . . It shall forevermore endure / The saints' and angels' song."

—*R. d.*

11. Who are the "sons of God" in Genesis 6?

Many people wonder about the statement that "the sons of God saw that the daughters of humans were beautiful, and they married any of them they chose" (Gen. 6:2). It is said that out of these unions came the Nephilim, a supposed race of giants that corrupted the earth (Gen. 6:4).

One view of Genesis 6:1–4 does indeed understand the passage as referring to the unions of fallen angels ("sons of God") with humanity ("daughters of man"), resulting in a race of giants on the earth. In fact, "sons of God" is used elsewhere as a title for angels (see Job 1:6 NASB). Moreover, some maintain that the New Testament affirms this interpretation when it speaks of "angels when they sinned" (2 Peter 2:4) and "did not keep their positions of authority but abandoned their proper dwelling" (Jude 6).

But there are some problems with this view. First, the phrase "sons of God" may mean angels but more frequently refers to humanity. Second, the New Testament passages more likely refer to angels following Satan in his rebellion against God and not marriage with women. Third, and most important, Jesus taught that angels were not capable of marriage and sexual reproduction (Matt. 22:30).

It seems better to understand Genesis 6:1–4 as referring to the intermarriage of the godly line of Seth and the ungodly line of Cain. The genealogies in the context support this interpretation. The text recounts the line of Cain, the first murderer (Gen. 4:17–24), immediately followed by the line of Seth (Gen. 4:25–5:32), a godly line from which "people began to call on the name of the LORD" (Gen. 4:26). After listing the two genealogies, Genesis 6:1–4 describes the uniting of these two groups (the sons of God and the daughters of man). The result of the merging of these two lines was the Nephilim, a Hebrew word that means "fallen ones," indicating that both lines were now corrupted. The older translation for these descendants was "giants," but a better translation is "heroes" or "powerful," indicating that they became infamous as "men of renown" (Gen. 6:4). It was their corrupting influence on the earth that led to God's judgment of the world by flood in Noah's day (Gen. 6:8–8:22).

Although Canaanites are called Nephilim later in Numbers 13:31–33, they were not the physical descendants of those in Genesis 6 because all humanity was destroyed in the flood that followed the corruption of the earth. Rather, the use of Nephilim in Numbers more likely identifies the Canaanites as a people who were corrupted and powerful.

—M. R.

23

12. First Samuel 16:13 says that Samuel anointed David, a young shepherd boy, to ultimately become Israel's king while he was in the presence of his brothers, and that the Spirit of the Lord came upon David from that day forward. But in the very next verse we read that the Spirit of God left Saul. I thought once the Spirit of God entered into us, He was always a part of us.

Actually, in the Old Testament, God's Spirit entered into people so that they could do some special task that they were given to accomplish. For example, when building the tabernacle and temple, God wanted the work to reflect His glory, and His Spirit entered the craftsmen.

Most believers agree that entrance of the Spirit of God into a believer's life after the resurrection is the divine seal of a born-again believer: "Do you not know that your bodies are temples of the Holy Spirit, who is in you, whom you have received from God?" (1 Cor. 6:19). The gift of the indwelling of the Spirit is the fulfillment of the promise of Jesus in John 14 to send a Comforter (see John 16:7–15).

—*M. K.*

13. I have always thought of God as someone who is on His throne in Heaven, keeping track of all the good and the bad things I've done. I've been a Christian for five years, and I know that I'm saved and His blood has cleansed me of all my sin, but I still see Him as looking for every flaw, uncovering another sin I've fallen into. How do I change how I feel about my relationship with God?

You are not alone. Many sincere believers have a wrong concept of God. They have carried all that they believed about God before their salvation into their lives today as believers. The basic problem is that they are looking to the wrong source for really knowing God and what we can expect of Him and what He expects of us. If you really want to know God, you need to study His own revelation of Himself through His Word, the Bible. Isaiah tells us that God is powerful, He is our Helper who "gives strength to the weary and increases the power of the weak" (40:29). God revealed the depths of His love when He became incarnate and dwelt among us as Jesus Christ the Lord.

As we read the Bible each day, we will see new and yet eternal descriptions of God that we have never comprehended before. Reading the Bible should always include the questions, "What does this Scripture say to us about God, and what does He expect us to do about it now?" Coming to know God as He really is presents one of the richest blessings that will transform our lives!

—M. K.

14. What does the letter to the Hebrews mean when it says Jesus "ascended into heaven" (Heb. 4:14)? At Jesus' ascension, did He go through outer space and the galaxies on the way to Heaven?

The writer to the Hebrews uses descriptions of the tabernacle in the Old Testament and the high priest's prescribed movement through the tabernacle on the Day of Atonement to communicate the transcendence of Christ's ascension into Heaven. Under the old covenant, the priests could enter the Holy Place for worship; but only the high priest could enter the Most Holy Place, and he could enter there only once a year on the Day of Atonement (Heb. 9:7). On the Day of Atonement, the high priest alone passed through the court of the tabernacle, went through the first compartment of the tabernacle, the Holy Place, then through the veil, and entered the Most Holy Place. He sprinkled the blood of atonement on and before the mercy seat, making the annual national atonement for Israel (see Lev. 16; Heb. 10:1).

The Lord Jesus did not pass through the earthly tabernacle, but He passed through the heavens. But we must not mistake the language of the tabernacle to mean that Jesus passed through outer space and through galaxies en route to Heaven. When Jesus ascended, a cloud received Him from the sight of His watching disciples, and the next moment He was in glory (see Acts 1:9–11). In a twinkling of an eye, Jesus transcended all the limits of time and space. He has taken His place at the right hand of God, the true Most Holy Place, and there He has made atonement for us—and unlike the atonement offered by the high priest in the tabernacle, His sacrifice is once for all and never needs to be repeated. What a wonder!

—*W. N.*

15. Lately, our Bible reading club has been reading the Old Testament with growing dismay. Its butchery appalls us, principally because it is attributed to God. God sends armies against helpless people with orders to slaughter them. God orders the indiscriminate killing of women and children. What gives? Is the God of the Old Testament different from the merciful God portrayed in the New Testament?

First, both the New and Old Testaments distinguish between God and gods (i.e., evil entities represented by idols and sometimes described as demons), but there is no distinction between the God of the Old Testament and the God of the New Testament. As the opening to the gospel of John declares, "In the beginning was the Word, and the Word was with God, and the Word was God. . . . The Word became flesh and made his dwelling among us. . . . No one has ever seen God, but the one and only Son, who is himself God . . . has made him known" (John 1:1, 14, 18). The apostle Paul develops the same truth in all his writings. If you know Christ, you know the Father in Heaven. What He was in Paul's time, He was in the ancient past and is forever—the unchanging God (Phil. 2:5–11; Col. 1:19; 2:9).

How then can we account for the descriptions of brutality

to which you refer? We must understand that God's character is always loving, gracious, just, and holy. God's judgment in response to pagan sins like child sacrifice accompanied His gracious rescue of people like Rahab (see Josh. 2; 6:17). This mixture of grace and justice is most clearly seen at the cross, when Jesus was crucified as the just penalty for our sins. Yet this act of judgment was also God's great act of love and salvation, making it possible for us to enter into fellowship with Him. The resurrection of Jesus vindicates the love and justice of God. We might not understand specific instances of how God has chosen to act. But our confidence must be in God's unchanging character, not in our own changing notions of what love and justice mean in the world.

—D. C.

16. How can we say that God promises to deliver and protect us when believers around the world are murdered and tortured? What are we protected and kept safe from? If He promises protection, then what does that protection mean?

Your question is timely, considering the world we are living in—indeed, the kind of world people have always lived in since the fall. It is also one of the harder questions to answer in any humanly satisfying way. As you have noted, Christians are the victims of violence, oppression, abuse, and deadly illness. The very famous volume *Foxe's Book of Martyrs* is full of stories of Christians who went to their deaths at the hands of wicked men and women. John and Betty Stam, who met and fell in love here at Moody Bible Institute, were beheaded by Communists while serving as missionaries in China. Yet, their baby daughter, hidden by her mother in a sleeping bag, was spared. Some are protected from violence; others are not.

There is a great deal of bad teaching on this subject, some of it sounding as though people are trying to get God off the hook for allowing suffering. People talk about God using evil to refine us and to draw us closer to Him, almost as though evil was necessary for God to accomplish His purposes. The truth is that God is not, in one author's words, "the secret architect of evil." He hates death and sin, and we are permitted to hate it too. The dark consequence of Adam and Eve's choice in the garden was that the relationship between men and women, between man and the earth, between men and women and God was broken. Sin entered in. Living in a damaged and decaying world, we are subject to its ills.

But as Romans 8:38–39 so beautifully reminds us, nothing "will be able to separate us from the love of God that is in Christ Jesus our Lord." He gives meaning to all that happens to us. As one theologian puts it, "Faith set us free from optimism long ago and taught us hope instead. . . . He will wipe away all tears from our eyes; there will be no more death, sorrow, crying or pain. He will sit on the throne; He will say, 'Behold I make all things new.'" This world is not the end of the story.

—R. d.

17. Did Jesus have grandparents?

Jesus' mother was a virgin; while she was engaged to Joseph, "before they came together, she was found to be pregnant through the Holy Spirit" (Matt. 1:18). During the time of the betrothal, Joseph kept her a virgin until after the birth of Jesus. Neither Joseph nor any other man contributed to the miraculous conception. Legally, however, Joseph was Jesus' father since he named Him (Matt. 1:21–25). Thus, Joseph's parents would have been considered Jesus' grandparents, and they would have had a legal connection to Him. Mary was the biological mother of Jesus, and so her parents would have also been His grandparents with a flesh-and-blood relationship to Him.

—*D. C.*

18. Where is it found that we should celebrate Jesus' birthday? It seems to me that Christians ought to celebrate His death more than His birth.

We mark the Lord's birth every year for at least three reasons: first, Scripture gives a lot of space to it. Jesus' birth is the subject of Old Testament prophecies, and two of the writers of the New Testament (Matthew and Luke) narrate the story in considerable detail.

Second, the birth is not just a sentimental story about a girl who was forced to have her baby in a barn, or about wise men riding into town on camels, or shepherds watching their flocks by night. It was the occasion when, Paul says, "God sent his Son, born of a woman, born under the law" (Gal. 4:4). That statement is just a sample from texts that brings us to the third reason for celebrating the birth of Jesus: its profound significance, summed up in the word *incarnation*.

That word means, as John says, "The Word became flesh. . . .

30

the one and only Son, who came from the Father, full of grace and truth" (John 1:14). The same paragraph adds, "No one has ever seen God, but the one and only Son, who is himself God . . . has made him known" (John 1:18).

Christmas is not about a mere baby. It is about God breaking into a broken world as a human being, in order to redeem lost humanity from sin's terrible consequences.

—D. C.

19. Do Christians, Jews, and Muslims all pray to the same God? The pope said we do, and in my conversations I find that people seem puzzled and divided on the issue.

The "same God" question is creating a lot of confusion in the Christian community. Pope Francis has asserted that Christians, Muslims, and Jews worship the same God, and Miroslav Volf—a prominent Protestant theologian—argues the same in his book *Do We Worship the Same God? Jews, Christians and Muslims in Dialogue.* The question also sparked a major controversy at Wheaton College when a tenured professor publicly espoused this view. The professor eventually resigned, but questions remain as to whether this view is compatible with orthodox Christian belief.

"Same God" proponents argue that there is enough overlap between ideas about God in the three religions to conclude that all three refer to the same deity. For example, Christians, Muslims, and Jews all acknowledge that there is one God, Creator of Heaven and earth, who will someday judge humanity. Proponents argue that when speaking to Muslims or Jews,

Christians can affirm that we all worship the same God, much like the apostle Paul did when speaking to the Athenians about their "UNKNOWN GOD" (see Acts 17:23).

Certainly, this argument has merit when considering whether Jews and Christians worship the same God. Christians can affirm the God of Judaism, for both religions embrace Yahweh as revealed in the Hebrew Scriptures. But like the "Unknown God," the Jewish concept of God is incomplete. It includes an accurate depiction of God the Father but fails to acknowledge Jesus, His Son.

A similar argument could be made for Allah prior to the sixth century and the creation of Islam. In ancient times, Allah was simply the Arabic name for God and literally meant "the God." But Muhammad transformed Allah from a vague concept of God into one that fundamentally contradicts the God of the Bible.

Though Islam recognizes Abraham and the prophets, Allah as described in the Quran is dramatically different from Yahweh. He is not love, but is capricious and sometimes cruel (cf. 1 John 4:8). And he is not our father but instead is distant and remote. Islam also recognizes Jesus, but only as a prophet, not as the Son of God (see 2 Cor. 1:2–3, 19). In fact, Muslims consider the Trinity to be blasphemy.

Additionally, tradition holds that Muhammad received his revelation about Allah from the angel Gabriel. But Scripture says that any spirit that denies Jesus as Christ is the antichrist (1 John 2:22) and that Satan "masquerades as an angel of light" (2 Cor. 11:14). Islam's origin might then be satanic, and to claim that Christians and Muslims worship the same God is not only a stretch, it's blasphemous. Allah is not an incomplete revelation of God; rather, he is an idol and a false god.

—J. R.

20. What do I do when it seems that God is moving too slowly in my life?

You are wise to use the word "seems." Humanly speaking, sometimes it does seem that God is taking too long to accomplish His purpose and carry out His promises in our lives. In a world of sound bites and nanoseconds, we followers of Christ have a vital lesson to learn: the importance and value of waiting on the Lord. The Lord is not in the business of producing microwave Christians. Spiritual growth takes time, and God is not in a rush. The Bible encourages us to wait on the Lord (see Pss. 27:14; 130:5–6).

God's people have often struggled with waiting on the Lord. Abraham and Sarah grew impatient and tired of waiting on the Lord; they took matters into their own hands, which didn't help (Gen. 16). I know that waiting on God at times is hard, and my heart goes out to you. But taking matters into our own hands is the worst thing that we can do. For example, if you are waiting on the Lord for a spouse and it seems that God is taking too long, the worst thing that you can do is lower biblical standards and marry outside of the mind and will of God. I want to encourage you to wait on the Lord. Don't run ahead of Him. Trust God and wait on His timing. If it seems that God is moving too slowly, it only seems that way. God is never late; He is always on time.

—W. N.

21. What does it mean in Exodus 7 and successive chapters when it says that God hardened Pharaoh's heart when Moses—speaking for God—asked him to "let my people go"? That doesn't sound terribly fair, does it?

This is a knotty question. Scholars have struggled with this for ages, including Jewish OT teachers. Some suggest that if God had actually hardened the leader of Egypt's heart, it was certainly His prerogative. God answers to no one. He is God, and He is sovereign. While that is true, I personally don't think He would treat Pharaoh any differently than He treats us. Second Peter 3:9 says, "He is patient with you, not wanting anyone to perish, but everyone to come to repentance."

Many Bible teachers suggest that Pharaoh hardened his own heart several times, at which point God hardened his heart terminally. Pharaoh's attitude toward the God of Israel and his refusal to submit to Him are seen in his words to Moses in Exodus 5:2: "Who is the LORD, that I should obey him and let Israel go? I do not know the LORD and I will not let Israel go."

His words echo the tone and rebellion of the vast majority of this world who blast God. Pharaoh refused Jehovah's claims, and ultimately his heart was hardened because of his failure to submit to his Creator.

Don't be stubborn and rebellious as Pharaoh and the Egyptians were. They wouldn't let Israel go until God had ravaged them with dreadful plagues. The question for us to answer is whether we are living like Pharaoh in our refusal to hear the

Word of God and submit to Him. We are exhorted in Hebrews 3:15, "Today, if you hear his voice, do not harden your hearts."
—*M. K.*

22. What does it mean to be filled with the Holy Spirit?

The best definition is "control." Jesus calls those who believe in Him to allow the Holy Spirit's control of their lives. Ephesians 5:18 uses the contrast between wine and the Holy Spirit—rather than be controlled ("drunk") with wine, we should be controlled ("filled") with the Spirit. Moreover, the Bible uses the same meaning of the word *filled* in other contexts. For example, Luke 5:26 speaks of people being "filled with awe." Acts 19:28 describes people as enraged or furious, meaning they are controlled by anger. The command to be filled with the Holy Spirit means that we are to be controlled by Him.

The real question is not what does it mean but how do we obey? We find the answer in Colossians, a book with a similar structure to the book of Ephesians. Colossians 3:16, a parallel passage to Ephesians 5:18, has a command followed by similar outcomes. In both passages, the results of obeying the command are worship, thanksgiving, and wholesome household relationships. But the command in Colossians 3:16 is different: "Let the message of Christ dwell among you richly." The word *dwell* was used of Roman troops forcibly occupying a conquered city. Therefore, the parallel command calls us to allow God's Word to take forcible occupation of our lives. We do this by reading, studying, meditating upon, and obeying God's Word. The results will be the same as the results of being filled with the Spirit. When God's Word takes forcible occupation of our lives, we are controlled by the Holy Spirit.

—*M. R.*

23. We Christians teach that Jesus died on Friday and rose on Sunday. There is no way you can get three days and three nights in the grave, which the Bible teaches (Matt. 12:39–41). So why do we teach it?

Many Bible students, including pastors, do *not* teach that Jesus died on Friday and rose on Sunday. They hold that He died on Wednesday or Thursday, and they defend their position in various ways. For example, some note that Jewish days began and ended at sundown, and that part of a day stood for an entire day.

Still others believe that the expression "three days and three nights" was, like "forty years in the wilderness," a literary device, not to be taken as meaning three twelve-hour days and three twelve-hour nights.

The weightiest argument against the Friday-to-Sunday position, I would judge, is the fact that the weekly Sabbath (the seventh day) was only one of several Sabbaths the people were commanded to observe. According to those who place great importance on this fact, in the Passover week of the year Jesus died, there were two Sabbath days—the weekly Sabbath and a Sabbath for the Passover. The assumption that there was only the weekly Sabbath (day seven) led to confusion about the time of Jesus' death.

What really matters is that for two millennia the Christian

world has held that Jesus died on Good Friday and rose from the dead on a Sunday morning, and much weighty scholarship defends the traditional view. We don't know the actual date of His birth, but we have celebrated it on December 25 for many years. In my mind, not knowing for sure on which day Jesus died does not negate the Christian observance of Good Friday, a time to remember the sacrifice that Jesus made for our sins.

—D. C.

24. Will Heaven be boring?

In *The Adventures of Huckleberry Finn*, Huck struggled with this very question, worried that he would "go around all day long with a harp and sing, forever and ever." Heaven sounded boring to Huck, compared to his life on earth.

But just imagine! The Bible describes Heaven as a city with streets of gold, built with rare jewels, and gates made of a single gigantic pearl. How can we even conceive of a place without a sun or moon, where "the glory of God gives it light" (Rev. 21:23)?

Think what it will be like to sit down with Abraham, Isaac, and Jacob, and others you've met in the pages of the Bible, asking them any questions we want (Matt. 8:11). Imagine a place where "'there will be no more death' or mourning or crying or pain" (Rev. 21:4).

On our journey, that is, in our lives here on earth, as we head for this amazing place we'll have trials, we'll grow discouraged, we'll encounter troubles and sorrow. But when we do, let's be comforted in this promise: "Our light and momentary troubles are achieving for us an eternal glory that far outweighs them all" (2 Cor. 4:17).

And the inheritance for those in Jesus Christ? Unlike any treasures on earth, this is one that "can never perish, spoil or fade. This inheritance is kept in heaven for you" (1 Peter 1:3–4). What awaits us is a dwelling that "has many rooms . . . I am going there to prepare a place for you," Jesus said (John 14:2).

Imagine all that! And now, know that Heaven will surpass anything we *can* imagine: "'What no eye has seen, what no ear has heard, and what no human mind has conceived'—the things God has prepared for those who love him" (1 Cor. 2:9).

That doesn't sound boring at all!

25. Often when we hear about the birth of our nation we hear that these Founding Fathers were believers. Recently I heard that some of these guys were what some call deists. So what's the difference between a deist and other Christians?

A deist is somebody who believes that God indeed created the world, but they say that all He did basically was to set it in motion and get it going like a clock. They suggest that from the point of creation until now God has operated with a hands-off policy. He doesn't intervene. Second Peter speaks of some who would come in the last days, scoffers walking after their own lusts, and saying "Where is this 'coming' he promised? Ever since our ancestors died, everything goes on as it has since the beginning of creation" (2 Peter 3:3–4).

These people ignore the fact that God has intervened in the

world of men both individually and corporately. He showed His power when He halted construction of the Tower of Babel, where He brought humiliating confusion to men's speech in a singular indictment of their pride. God also intervened in the lives of sinful men who needed a Savior by providing His own Son as the only acceptable sacrifice for sin. There is no way that a discerning reader can open the Bible and not see God's hand in the lives of people.

In contrast, a genuine man or woman of faith is described in Hebrews 11:6: "And without faith it is impossible to please God, because anyone who comes to him must believe that he exists and that he rewards those who earnestly seek him." Not only does God exist, but He is a personal God who has a purpose for each of us. You can't get much more personal than that. It is commendable to believe in a god who creates the world—but it's not enough.

—*M. K.*

26. I am puzzled by the idea that at Communion we eat Jesus' body and drink His blood. How can that be true?

It is true figuratively, not literally. There would be no confusion about the matter if we don't isolate a few verses in John 6 from the rest of the chapter. Jesus said, "Whoever eats my flesh and drinks my blood has eternal life, and I will raise them up at the last day. For my flesh is real food and my blood is real drink" (John 6:54–55). But that is not all He said about the subject.

That Jesus did not intend to be taken literally is clear from the rest of the chapter. His enemies introduced the subject of bread (manna). Moses produced it miraculously, they claimed. So what can *you* do to prove that you came from God? Jesus replied that He was the true bread from Heaven: "Whoever comes to me will never go hungry, and whoever believes in me will never be thirsty" (v. 35). In the verses that follow, He says repeatedly that he or she who *believes* will have eternal life. Thus, eating and drinking must be understood as metaphors for coming to Him in faith.

—*D. C.*

27. Why did God create drugs and abortion or even sin?

First, let's dismiss from our minds the thought that God creates now or ever did create sin in general or specific sins such as abortion or murder or kidnapping. Many examinations of the possibility that God is the author of sin have been done already, thousands of times, and are available in nearly every church library. God is never the source of evil, nor does He ever tempt anyone to sin (James 1:13).

Drugs are a different kind of issue, assuming that you are thinking mainly about street drugs. Drugs available at pharmacies are often life-saving. At a minimum, they ease our pain. Three cheers for aspirin! Street drugs, on the other hand, are often regular drugs prepared in licensed pharmaceutical laboratories, intended to be controlled by prescriptions and filled by licensed pharmacists. But they have escaped legal control and fallen into the hands of dealers or other species of malevolent merchandisers. Such dealers peddle them—they sell them to addicts or soon-to-be-addicts who have no prescriptions. They might not even be aware of the potential harm in medicines that, while giving a high (a briefly pleasant sensation), could harm or even kill them.

The street peddlers and their customers alike operate outside the law, and what they do is destructive, which is why the *illegal* drug trade is illegal. It is managed by robbers, manipulators, and even murderers.

How can God be accused of complicity with this dirty business? Actually, I think what causes the root of your concern is God's apparent passivity in the presence of evil. How can He stand idly by while the devil wreaks havoc in the world?

That is a fair question, and a short answer is that we don't always know His purposes and will. But we do know His character: "Every good and perfect gift is from above, coming down from the Father of the heavenly lights, who does not change like shifting shadows. He chose to give us birth through the word of truth" (James 1:17–18).

It isn't God who messes up the world with noxious, toxic chemicals. As the apostle Paul says, God gives us "rain from heaven and crops in their seasons; he provides you with plenty of food and fills your hearts with joy" (Acts 14:17).

Drug dealers are predators; they feed on society's most vulnerable members. As for participation in the business, consider Galatians 5:19–21. The word translated "witchcraft" in the English Bible is, in the Greek text, *pharmakeos*, from *pharmakeon*, meaning "a spellbinding potion; a druggist (pharmacist) or poisoner, i.e., (by extension) a magician, sorcerer" (see *Strong's Exhaustive Concordance of the Bible*).

I ask again how God can be suspected of having any part in

this devilish business. But he who gives healing drugs is neither poisoner nor sorcerer.

—*D. C.*

28. Since the Lord never tempts His people, why does Jesus instruct us in the model prayer to pray, "Lead us not into temptation" (Matt. 6:13)?

God's holy character is at the heart of this question. In His goodness and wisdom, God tests us to bring out the best in us or to reveal to us His character and provision in our lives (see Genesis 22 and the book of Job). But He never tempts us to do evil (James 1:13–15). Satan and our sinful natures are the sources of our temptations (see Matt. 4:1–11; 1 Thess. 3:5)

In the Lord's Prayer, described by some as the model prayer, after we have asked for forgiveness, we ask our heavenly Father not to lead us into those things that cause us to yield to temptation in the first place. We ask our heavenly Father to keep us from anything that will bring us into sin, any temptation that will result in us yielding to sin. We are not asking for exemption from all temptation. We want God's protection from temptations that we cannot handle.

Jesus further connects prayers and deliverance from temptation in Mark 14:38: "Watch and pray so that you will not fall into temptation. The spirit is willing, but the flesh is weak." When our hearts are filled with holy desire to honor the Lord in our lives, we seek to avoid falling into sin. We follow the instruction of Jesus to pray for the Father's guidance and the

Spirit's power to deliver us from temptations that would over-come us.

This request should be on our lips every day! And according to 1 Corinthians 10:13, our faithful God will always provide a way for us to escape any temptation we cannot handle. He delights to answer this prayer. When we yield to temptation we have no one to blame but ourselves.

—*W. N.*

29. I have a terrible time believing that God can actually forgive me. I know what the Bible says, but I feel so defeated. My memories are loaded with so many things that keep coming back to haunt my fellowship with God. How can God forgive me when I can't let go of all this guilt and shame?

We know that it's hard to believe when negative thoughts threaten to overwhelm you. But the truth is that God and His mediator Jesus Christ tell you that He will remember your sins no more (Isa. 43:25). God will no longer bring up your sins to indict you. He will not torment you with guilt and shame over your past sins. They have been forgiven by Christ, who bore each of those sins on His cross (1 Peter 2:24).

God's promise of forgiveness is truth, and the litany of shame in your mind is not. None of us feels worthy of His forgiveness, and we are not. We are not forgiven because we deserve it! But God, because of Christ, has forgiven you. Look through a concordance at all the references to forgiveness and realize that they are all talking about you. What a joy! Seize the truth. Let it inspire you. Memorize these verses and make them yours.

—*M. K.*

30. Is it true that "God helps those who help themselves"? Someone said this is not in the Bible, and that it was Benjamin Franklin who said it.

Benjamin Franklin, in his *Poor Richard's Almanac*, penned many memorable maxims that to this day exercise a profound influence on American culture. These maxims include "He that lies down with dogs, shall rise up with fleas," "Haste makes waste," and yes, "God helps them that help themselves." Actually, Franklin was not the originator of that last one; about two centuries earlier, Sidney Algernon in his *Discourses Concerning Government* said, "God helps those who help themselves."

It may surprise some to learn that these well-known words are not in the Bible. I appreciate the thinking behind that statement, but it is not an accurate statement of biblical truth. Romans 5:6 declares, "For while we were still *helpless*, at the right time Christ died for the ungodly" (NASB, italics added). We are not able to bring ourselves into a right relationship with God! The helpless human family stands in need of divine help and aid.

I am grateful that God helps the helpless who trust and rely on His Son. On the other hand, the fact that we cannot save ourselves is not a call for us as Christians to be passive in life. We are commanded to devote ourselves to prayer (Col. 4:2), to love and serve one another (1 John 4:7; Gal. 5:13), to control our tongues (Eph. 4:29; James 3:1–12), to hold a job (Eph.

4:28), and to raise our children for the glory of God (Deut. 6:6–7; Eph. 6:4). Of course, God enables us to do these things, but we must cooperate with Him in the process of living out the Christian life.

Further, there are some things that God is not going to come down from Heaven and do. The Lord will not punch the clock for us, nor will He mow our lawns and balance our checkbooks. The Lord will not attend class for us, nor will He do our homework. God expects us to do these things and He enables us to do them. Therefore, we give the Lord the glory for saving us, we give Him the glory for enabling us to obey Him, and we give Him the glory for blessing and confirming the work of our hands.

—*W. N.*

31 The Scriptures teach that the Messiah will be the Prince of Peace, but Jesus said, "Do not suppose that I have come to bring peace to the earth. I did not come to bring peace, but a sword" (Matt. 10:34). How can Jesus be called the Prince of Peace and promise that His coming will result in war?

There are several elements to understanding this unexpected passage. To begin, the Lord Jesus knew that His words would be viewed as controversial. Second, the word "sword" is figurative, not literal. The Lord was not saying He would bring war; rather, He would bring division. Third, the context is about family relations, not different nations. Faith in Jesus as the Messiah would bring division to families: "For I have come to turn 'a man against his father, a daughter against her mother'" (Matt. 10:35).

Finally, this passage is predictive, not prescriptive. It foresees that faith in Jesus will divide families but does not demand that it do so. For example, my own faith in Jesus caused my father to disown me despite my desire to maintain our relationship. But I could not restore a relationship with him without giving up my faith in Jesus. Jesus called me to love Him even more than my own father (Matt. 10:37).

—*M. R.*

32. Does God kill children as punishment for their parents' sins? I read somewhere that the sins of the parents are passed on to the third generation. Eight years ago, my son died in an auto accident, and I still struggle with this question.

No, God does not kill children—not to punish them for having bad parents, and not to punish their parents. The general principle is that each of us answers to God for our own sin, and for ours alone. Study Ezekiel 18, a critically important chapter intended to correct a false understanding of the "sins of the fathers."

After Jesus Christ died on the cross, He provided something the Old Testament believers did not have—forgiveness for all sins past, present, and future. God does not want believers to sin, but if we do, "we have an advocate with the Father—Jesus Christ, the Righteous One," who is "the atoning sacrifice for our sins, and not only for ours but also for the sins of the whole world" (1 John 2:1–2). One who believes in Jesus Christ does not need to fear a punishment for sins—Jesus has already paid the penalty.

—D. C.

33. Where did Jesus' spirit go between Good Friday and Resurrection Sunday? Did Jesus go to Hell?

The idea that the Lord Jesus went to Hell between the crucifixion and the resurrection, frequently called "the harrowing of Hell," has been believed since ancient times. In fact, the Apostles' Creed seems to teach it when it says, "He suffered under Pontius Pilate, was crucified, died and was buried; he descended into hell; on the third day he rose again from the dead."

The earliest versions of the creed omit the phrase "he descended into hell." The belief in the harrowing of Hell is based on the misinterpretation of several passages. Ephesians 4:9 says that the Lord Jesus "descended to the lower, earthly regions." But this refers to the incarnation, when the Son of God became a man, not a descent to Hell. First Peter 3:19–20 says, "He went and made proclamation to the imprisoned spirits—to those who were disobedient long ago when God waited patiently in the days of Noah." This is not talking about preaching in Hell; rather, the passage refers to Jesus preaching through Noah in the past to people who were alive in the days of Noah. Because they rejected Noah's message, they are now "imprisoned spirits."

Finally, John 20:17 records Jesus' words to Mary Magdalene: "Do not hold on to me, for I have not yet ascended to the

Father." This is not saying that Jesus' spirit had not yet been to His Father, but rather that Mary should stop clinging to the Lord Jesus because His bodily ascension was yet to come. In other words, Jesus is saying, *You can let go of me, Mary. I will be with you for the next forty days because I have not yet made my final ascension to the Father* (cf. Acts 1:9–11).

The Scriptures teach that when the physical body of the Lord Jesus died, His spirit went to His Father immediately. In Luke 23:43, Jesus assures the criminal on the cross: "Today you will be with me in paradise." Luke 23:46 records the Lord Jesus' words at the point of death:

"Father, into your hands I commit my spirit."

—M. R.

34. How I can have faith in God's promises when people break their promises all the time?

So many people tell us to believe them. We go to a store, and the salesman tells us his product is the greatest, the cheapest, and has the longest warranty. We buy it and take it home, and within days we realize it's another case of misplaced trust. Politicians constantly make promises that they can't possibly keep. People even make promises from the pulpit, claiming that they can grow the church or solve the budget problems or change the community. But pastors and church leaders can disappoint us when they make promises beyond the reliable truth found in the Word of God.

Only Jesus can say, "I am the way and the truth and the life. No one comes to the Father except through me" (John

14:6). As the book of Numbers tells us, "God is not human, that he should lie, not a human being, that he should change his mind. Does he speak and then not act? Does he promise and not fulfill?" (Num. 23:19). Unlike salesmen, politicians, preachers—and all people—everything that God says is good and true and can be trusted. He never makes a promise that He cannot or will not keep.

—*M. K.*

35. My wife and I have been having an ongoing discussion concerning the practice of meditation. My belief is that it is of no use to either Christians or nonbelievers in seeking God's will, knowing God better, or discovering His direction in any particular matter. Can you please help us understand this better?

I am glad that you and your wife are having a discussion about the practice of meditation. With the rise of interest in spirituality and Eastern mysticism in Western culture, you are not the only ones having an ongoing discussion about this practice.

It is critical, however, that we do not confuse Eastern meditation with biblical meditation. In Eastern or transcendental meditation, a person attempts to empty the mind of thought in order to be detached mentally and emotionally from the physical world for the purpose of becoming one with the so-called cosmic consciousness. The switch of active mental effort is turned off, and a person is consequently exposed to whatever external impressions may come. The practice is fraught with danger. In this passive frame of mind, a person may be open to satanic and demonic powers and influences.

On the other hand, biblical meditation is rigorous and prolonged reflection and thought about the person of God, the character of God, the ways of God, and the Word of God. In biblical meditation a person takes a portion of Scripture and thinks hard about the passage, reflecting slowly and deeply about the content of the passage and its practical implications for living. In biblical meditation a person is in an active frame of mind, filling the mind with the Scriptures.

The Lord wants us to meditate, filling our minds with His Word. The Lord Himself commands Joshua to habitually meditate on His Word: "This book of the law shall not depart from your mouth, but you shall meditate on it day and night" (Josh. 1:8 NASB). Habitual meditation on the Word of God is one of the hallmarks of the blessed person in Psalm 1:2. The banks of Psalm 63:1–8 are overflowing with the river of David's desire for God Himself! Since God has been his help and David finds joy under the shadow of the Lord's wings, he remembers God on his bed, and meditates upon God in the night watches. I find it interesting that the setting here is night and David is in bed. Instead of allowing his mind to wander into the dark woods of faulty thinking, David fills his mind with thoughts of God. He gives lengthy and prolonged mental consideration to God's person, character, and ways. The Psalms have much to say about the practice of biblical meditation (see Pss. 1:2; 4:4; 63:6; 104:34; 119:15, 23, 48, 78, 97, 99, 148; 143:5–6).

Deep and prolonged thinking about the Lord's Word, person, and work is biblical and is an integral part of our responsibility as Christians. Realizing the biblical mandate to think deeply about God and His Word, Christians have practiced biblical meditation for centuries, but our generation has mostly forgotten the vital place that meditation holds in Christian thinking and living. Meditation is important because whatever is shaping our thinking is shaping our lives and our characters. Reflection on the Scriptures allows God's Word to penetrate the inner caverns of our minds and our emotions, to soften our hard hearts and wills. In biblical meditation we cultivate the habit of thinking about Him who matters most in life.

In answering this question, I also want to give some suggestions to help with the practice of biblical meditation. First, in your regular reading of the Bible, take a verse or a portion of a verse and read it slowly and live with the verse through the day. You might take the words, "The LORD is my shepherd" and ponder them through the day. If you wake up at night and can't sleep, go over these words in your mind. Instead of turning on the television or radio or going online, try meditating on God's Word. Second, every day reflect on one of God's attributes. For example, you might reflect on God's wisdom on Monday, His omnipotence on Tuesday, and so on. Make your reflection a part of your prayers and praise God for the attribute that you are considering. Over time your experiential knowledge of God will increase. You will not only know more about the Lord, but you will actually get to know Him better!

For more in depth reading about the vital practice of biblical meditation, I suggest that you pick up Richard Foster's book *Celebration of Discipline*. For help with daily meditation on our Lord Himself, I would strongly encourage you to read

Knowledge of the Holy by A. W. Tozer and *Knowing God* by J. I. Packer. May your meditation be blessed!

—W. N.

36. Some people say God knows everything about us. If God already knows everything, why do we need to pray for ourselves and others?

It is true that God knows from all eternity everything about us. He called us to Himself in the infinite knowledge of everything that was against us and in the infinite knowledge of everything we would think, feel, and experience in this life! In virtue of His eternality, the Lord has already lived all our tomorrows as well as our yesterdays. Still, Scripture encourages us on numerous occasions to pray (Luke 18:1; Eph. 6:18; Col. 4:2–3; 1 Thess. 5:17; Jude 20). But it is clear from Scripture that prayer is not the tool we employ to inform our heavenly Father about our needs, problems, and struggles. The Bible says, "Your Father knows what you need before you ask him" (Matt. 6:8). Before we express any need to God, He already knows it.

Philippians 4:6 does say, "Present your requests to God." This command may give the impression that God is uninformed about our requests and needs; that, however, is not what the passage is saying. Rather, we can tell God about all our problems, needs, and struggles and make requests accordingly. Prayer is communication with our heavenly Father who cares for us, listens to us, and understands us. Since He already knows what our needs are before we pray to Him, our prayers are really a practical demonstration of our dependence on Him and our faith in Him. We pray not to inform God, but because we trust Him, need Him, and long to talk with Him! God the Father delights when we trust Him and cast all our anxieties on Him.

The fact that God knows everything before we pray ought to fill us with immense encouragement to pray. We don't have to decide if we are going to inform God about our pain, struggles, temptations, anxieties, and fear, because He already knows these things. The issue is whether we in faith will talk to Him about these issues. So I want to encourage you. Trust your heavenly Father, have that talk with Jesus, and tell Him about all your problems (1 Peter 5:7).

—*W. N.*

37. Is it possible for us to ask God for too much in prayer?

Thankfully, no! The Bible says that God "is able to do immeasurably more than all we ask or imagine" (Eph. 3:20). Paul is not saying, however, that we can expect God to grant us whatever we ask. We are instructed to pray according to God's will and His Word and in submission to Christ. Still, we should be encouraged. We should be bold in our prayers, confident to ask God to do the impossible (see Heb. 4:16). No request is too great for God (see Jer. 32:27). Nothing is impossible with Him! Nothing is too hard for Him. It is not a question of God's power; it is a question of His will and wisdom (see Dan. 3:16–18).

—*W. N.*

38. Why did God use the form of a story to give us so much of the truth in the Bible?

Much of Scripture is historical narrative, a genre that tells history in the form of story. I believe the Lord communicated a major part of His revelation in the Old and New Testaments in historical narrative/story for several reasons. First, story is universal; second, story is memorable; third, stories have the power to penetrate our minds before our sinful defense systems rise up against the truth; and fourth, stories appeal to our imaginations. The God who created us knows that we are more than just rational brains; we also have hearts and emotions that respond to the wondrous story of His love for His people.

Yes, God is the great storyteller, the ultimate communicator of truth through story. But there is more: through faith in Christ our story becomes a part of His incredible story of redemption.

—*W. N.*

39. When I was diagnosed as suffering from clinical depression, I asked the therapist, "Why does not God intervene?" She said, "He does! The staff and I are His intervention." What do you think?

I am inclined to agree with her. God works through people, and if she and her staff helped you, as you clearly imply in your letter, you can take the help as from the Lord and thank Him.

In response to King Hezekiah's mournful prayer when he was told that he was dying, God granted him fifteen more years of life. The king would recover, but only through the ministrations of a prophet sent by God. The prophet Isaiah ordered that a poultice of figs be applied to Hezekiah's nearly fatal boil, and Hezekiah recovered. Obviously, the Lord stopped the king's lurching toward death. But He didn't just say "Get well!" He sent Isaiah with a few figs for medical intervention (Isa. 38:21–22).

—D. C.

40. After going to church for most of my life, last night I heard for the first time that Christ created Heaven and earth. If this is correct, why isn't it taught in Christian churches?

Most biblical references to creation speak of God as the Creator, as in Genesis 1:1: "In the beginning God created the heavens and the earth" (see also Acts 17:24–31). The New Testament narrows the focus to God the Son, and speaks of Him as the Creator. See John 1:3, 10: "Through him all things were made; without him nothing was made that has been made . . . [and] the world was made through him." In his letter to new believers in Colossae, Paul states this truth just as forcefully as does John: "For in him [the Son of God] all things were created: things in heaven and on earth, visible and invisible, whether thrones or powers or rulers or authorities; all things were created through him and for him" (Col. 1:16).

If this truth is not taught in churches you attend, it's possible that important texts are being neglected.

—D. C.

41. Once one becomes a believer and is indwelt by the Holy Spirit, is it possible for an evil spirit that may have taken up residence in that soul to still remain?

When an individual places his or her faith in the work of Christ on the cross, the apostle Paul writes that God has bought that one with the blood of His Son (1 Cor. 6:20). The mark of authenticity that indicates that we belong to God is the indwelling of the Holy Spirit (Eph. 1:13–14). Finally, John tells us in his first epistle that the one who indwells us is greater than the evil spirits who are in the world (1 John 4:4).

Putting these verses together, I believe that any individual who comes to Christ has become a new creature. This means that all the old things have passed away, and God who now owns us, is in the process of making all things new (2 Cor. 5:17). In order to do it, He gifts us with the Holy Spirit, who becomes God's seal of ownership. And since the Holy Spirit is greater than any evil spirit who may have occupied this individual in his old way of life, and since God does not share ownership, no evil spirit can remain in residence once conversion occurs.

This does not mean, however, that believers cannot open themselves to demonic influences because of poor or evil choices that they make in life. Our experience of the Holy Spirit's renewal of our lives requires our faith in God's goodness and in His love. But as long as the individual continues to affirm the name of Christ (see 2 Tim. 2:12), I do not believe an evil spirit can take permanent residence in the life of a believer.

—*D. R.*

42. Wasn't the Lord Jesus supposed to be the perfect model of love? Why did He call the Canaanite woman a dog (Matt. 15:21–28)?

At first glance, it does seem rude to compare this woman to a dog. But Jesus' words actually are gentle. He used the word *kunarion*, which means "puppy, house pet," not the word *kuon* for "wild, pack dogs." Moreover, Jesus was expressing God's divine priority, not bigotry. As the Messiah of Israel, He needed to minister to the Jewish people first. Finally, the woman did not take offense but rather accepted God's divine priority. In the end, the Lord Jesus commended her faith and healed her daughter, showing that the Messiah would respond to humble faith from anyone, Jewish or Gentile.

—*M. R.*

43. What does the divine name "I AM" in Exodus 3:14 mean?

If the Bible is a story, then the major character is obviously God. An important question you can ask of God is what Moses asked, "What is his name?" (Ex. 3:13). A name is a window to the soul of the person. In Exodus 3 we get an answer to this question, but there are many interpretations of what this name means. It is not an exaggeration to say that the three Hebrew words that are translated "I AM WHO I AM" have been discussed more than any other phrase in the entire Old Testament. Let me list three possibilities.

The first option is to see in this name God's absolute self-sufficiency. God is the self-existent one. He has life within Himself. In the language of Isaiah, He is the Alpha and the Omega, the self-sustaining one. It is impossible for God not to exist. And this God does not depend on anyone or anything. Nothing outside of God can affect Him in any sense; He is utterly unconditioned.

The second option translates the name of God as, "I make to be whatever comes to be." God is the one who causes all things into being. If the first option references the eternality of God, the second option speaks of His creative power. He is the one who has created all things; He is the one who sustains all things. In the language of Isaiah, God does not grow weary or tired, for He is the Creator of the ends of the earth (Isa. 40:28).

The third option sees the emphasis within the name of God as His active presence. He is Immanuel, the one who is with us. Or, to put it another way, He is the one who was with Abraham, Isaac, and Jacob. In the language of Isaiah, He is the God who lives in the high and lofty place, but dwells among the contrite and lowly in spirit. If the first possibility references the eternality of God, the second His power, then the third speaks of the God's desire for relationship with humanity.

While all three interpretations are obviously true of God, and all three have strong support, the third possibility seems best. It fits the context quite well. The Israelites had been suffering in Egypt as slaves for many generations, and Exodus 3 notes that God sees their pain, hears their cry, and is concerned with their misery. When Moses arrives to deliver them, and they ask him what is God's name, the name "I Am" answers that very question: I have been with you in the midst of your suffering.

Such an interpretation also aligns perfectly with the life of Jesus, who is God with us, to suffer together with us and for us. The hour of glory in the life of Christ is the hour of His suffering on the cross for our sake. The cross is the window to the divine soul because in the cross His name shines the brightest.

—D. R.

44. I've been wrestling with how much God should be involved in my pursuit of holiness and how much is up to me. I feel frustrated with the seeming contradiction people display when they at once say it's only by the grace of God that they were freed from sin yet so often emphasize striving to be good.

It is both. It is only by the grace of God that we can even begin to choose what is good, but God did not save us to be robots. I once heard a pastor say that at times we see ourselves as much too passive in our Christian walk. He added that when we respond to God and invite Him onto the throne of our lives, He doesn't ask us to step down but invites us to join Him to do our part under His authority.

While God's grace gives us the impetus to respond, we always have the choice to say yes or no. We couldn't even begin the process of holiness without God's pursuing grace, or maintain holiness in our lives without Him. However, we are responsible for using our will to choose what is right in that maintenance.

Striving is really the wrong word; submission—which is a purposeful, decisive act of the will, not a flaccid surrender—is more accurate. The book of James presents well the tension that exists in a believer's life. One powerful statement reads, "As the body without the spirit is dead, so faith without deeds is dead" (2:26).

—R. d.

45. I am confused. Doesn't 2 Corinthians 5:10 contradict Psalm 103:3 and Isaiah 53:5–6? If Jesus died for us, why is He going to judge us and punish us for our sins?

There is no contradiction. The texts in the Old Testament state clearly that God forgives us our sins. He is a forgiving God. Isaiah bases free forgiveness on the sacrifice of the Substitute, whom we know to be Jesus. Second Corinthians and other texts like it (e.g., Rom. 14:12; 1 Cor. 3:8–15) deal with God's evaluation of us after having forgiven us and brought us into His family. Now, He deals with us "as his children" (Heb. 12:7).

The issue for us believers is not salvation; it is rewards, and it is God's approval or the withholding of approval. There is no question about the permanency of our salvation. "There is now no condemnation for those who are in Christ Jesus" (Rom. 8:1), but there will be an examination of their lives as forgiven sinners.

—D. C.

46. I have tried to find a Scripture reference to explain the use of "in Jesus' name" we pray at the end of prayers and can only come up with all the references to doing everything "in His name," which of course would include praying. Could you please give your thoughts on the subject?

On the night that He was betrayed, Jesus instructed His disciples—and by implication His people throughout history—to pray in His name. To see how Jesus emphasized this point, read John 14:13–24.

Praying in the name of Jesus generally is interpreted to mean that we simply add the words "in the name of Jesus" or "for Jesus' sake" at the end of our prayers. These precious encouragements to pray in the name of Jesus are understood in this way because today people in the Western world do not think of names the way people thought of them in the ancient world. Today we give people names to distinguish them from one another, whereas in the ancient world a name represented a person—his character, nature, all that he was. In the Scriptures, the name of God stands for the totality—a summary representation—of God's person, nature, and character.

To pray in Jesus' name does not mean that we just add the words "in Jesus' name" at the end of our prayers. Praying in this way reduces prayer to a formula. To pray in Jesus' name means that we pray in a way that is in harmony with Jesus' character, person, and nature. It means that we pray with attitudes and a heart disposition that are consistent with the attitudes and heart disposition of Jesus—faith in God the Father, reverence for God's person, and willingness to submit to God's will. Of course, it is okay to add "in the name of Jesus" at the end of our prayers as long as we know what we are doing and understand the implications of the words. Still, we can pray in Jesus' name without tacking the words on as some kind of spiritual formula at the end of our prayers. The Lord is concerned with the condition of our heart and the quality of our attitudes in prayer (Ps. 66:18–19; James 4:3).

—W. N.

47. Two questions: First, I was hit by a hit-and-run driver. How can I forgive him if I do not know who he is? Second question: if God is a God of justice, why does He allow that driver to get away with what he did to me? I never received a dollar in compensation. All those passages Paul wrote look good on paper, but that is about as far as they go.

Here is a three-part answer: First, you need to "get rid of all bitterness" (Eph. 4:31). Bitterness will spoil your soul. Second, you don't need to know the scoundrel who ran into you and ran away. All you need is the example of Christ, who prayed for a mob of nameless, faceless people who were leading Him to the cross, "Father, forgive them, for they do not know what they are doing" (Luke 23:34). Peter reminds us that Jesus "entrusted himself to him who judges justly" (1 Peter 2:23).

That brings us to the third part: Justice is God's prerogative. He will take care of that hit-and-run driver as He likes, when

He likes. Justice will be done. Meanwhile, let's thank God that in His mercy you were not killed by the incident.

—D. C.

48. If I understand and embrace the doctrine of election, does it stop me from praying for unsaved people?

Even for those who acknowledge election as a biblical doctrine, the concept might conjure up pictures of a capricious or biased God. But rightly understood, election refers to an act of God in eternity, according to the good pleasure of His sovereign freedom, and on account of no foreseen merit in sinful people, whereby He chooses, in mercy, to save some individuals on the basis of the person and work of Jesus Christ alone. The doctrine of election does underscore that some people are saved and some people will not be saved, and it has been a troubling and confusing teaching for some people.

The narrative of God bringing redemption to the world through Christ is a story about God's choices to bring certain people into the line of promise. He selected Abraham from a family of idol worshipers; He chose Isaac rather than Ishmael; He loved Jacob and not Esau (see Gen. 21:12–13; Josh. 24:2; Mal. 1:2–3). Abraham experienced salvation because of God's choice, while many in Abraham's family did not experience salvation. Ishmael received blessing in this life in keeping with God's promise to his mother, Hagar, to preserve his life, but he did not experience the salvation and gift of inheritance promised to Isaac. God's love for Jacob placed Jacob in the line of promise, but Esau was not included in the promise of salvation.

From Jacob, God called out the twelve tribes of Israel, of whom He says: "The LORD did not set his affection on you and choose you because you were more numerous than other peoples, for you were the fewest of all peoples. But it was because the LORD loved you and kept the oath he swore to your ancestors that he brought you out with a mighty hand and redeemed you from the land of slavery, from the power of Pharaoh king of Egypt" (Deut. 7:7–8). The Lord's choice to redeem Israel for salvation out of all other nations is an intentional choice of God's great love alone.

The apostle Paul draws on the Old Testament story of Israel in order to acquit God of accusations of injustice for choosing to save some in Israel rather than all in Israel (see Rom. 9:6–18). First, Paul indicates that God's distinction of the children of promise from children of the flesh shows that His word has not failed toward Israel. God's purpose in election is demonstrated because the "older" Esau serves the "younger" Jacob. Jacob will continue the line of promise of the covenant blessings given to Abraham and Isaac.

Second, Paul reveals that God's freedom to give mercy as He wills, as in the case of Pharaoh, acquits Him of injustice in election. God owes no one mercy, for all people are sinners before Him; all are deserving of the wrath Pharaoh experienced. The gift of mercy is God's free choice to withhold judgment from some rather than others. Without such mercy, not one person would experience salvation. Mercy is not a matter of justice or injustice.

God's choice to save people in mercy invites rather than limits our prayers for unsaved people. Paul exhorted the church to pray for governing authorities: "This is good, and pleases

God our Savior, who wants all people to be saved and to come to a knowledge of the truth" (1 Tim. 2:3–4). We pray for the hope of salvation of lost persons through Christ the Redeemer.

—E. C. R.

49. If God loves the world and wants each person to be saved, then why doesn't He make this happen? For example, I have a friend who seems to sincerely search for God, yet he says that there just isn't enough convincing evidence out there for him to make a choice for God. Why didn't God provide more evidence?

This question touches on one of the most difficult issues in religious discussions today. Some atheists argue that the presence of unpersuaded genuine seekers of God is itself evidence that either God does not possess the power to make Himself more evident or that God does not truly desire the salvation of all. The common analogy used is of a child playing hide-and-seek with his mother. Somehow the child gets lost in the woods behind the backyard. He figures that sooner or later his mother will come searching for him out there. But after hours of wandering, his mother is nowhere in sight. When he cries out "Mom!" there is no response. Nighttime comes, and still no evidence of Mom.

The parallels are obvious. God is the mom who desires to reach out and save those who are lost. While a human mom may have had a heart attack or gotten entangled in another part of the woods, a divine Father would certainly have the power to bring about a reunion. What are we to think of a

Father who has the ability but does not seem to expend the energy necessary? Could it be that He doesn't even exist?

Christian scholars have offered a number of responses to this argument. Some say that if the seeker was truly genuine and sincere, God would have revealed Himself to them. After all, Jeremiah promises that the one who seeks God with all his heart will find him (29:13). James seems to affirm this promise in the New Testament: "Come near to God and he will come near to you" (4:8). When someone wants to find God and know God, and not merely experience the benefits, then surely he will find God. Other scholars argue that if God reveals Himself without constraint, the individual would be so overwhelmed by His presence that his freedom to enter into a relationship with God would be negated.

While there may be something to both of these responses, there is another possibility. Evidence can come in several forms: arguments for God such as the complexity and specificity of life pointing to a designer; a miracle such as a resurrection or a healing; divine presence as in a dream or a visionary experience. But there is one more kind of evidence: divine presence in the church. What if the church is to show God to the world? The way the church lives out its own gospel would determine how much evidence there is for God's existence. Jesus Himself said that if we love one another as He has loved us, the world will know that He has sent us (John 13:34–35; 17:23).

—D. R.

50. What is your view of veneration of or devotion to the Virgin Mary?

I see no evidence in Scripture that the mother of Jesus or the saints (as defined by the Roman Catholic Church) were to be venerated. When Cornelius fell on his knees before Peter, Peter yanked him to his feet, saying, "Stand up. I am only a man myself" (Acts 10:26). Later, Paul and Barnabas were aghast at worship (or veneration) offered them. They tore their clothes in dismay (Acts 14:8–18). The thrust of the ministry of the apostles, whether by word or in their writings, was to direct worship to the Lord Himself.

True, Mary was blessed. She was given special favor: to be the mother of Jesus. But there is no suggestion anywhere in Scripture that she should receive homage, veneration, devotion, or worship. That should be directed to our risen Lord.

Veneration and other forms of devotion raise another problem: seeking guidance or information from Mary and the saints detracts from the authority of Scripture. God speaks to us through the Word. What should be said about "messages" from sources other than the Bible, especially if they conflict with plain statements in God's Word?

—D. C.

51. I'm not sure how to keep Christ in Christmas, since it has become so commercialized. I've heard some of the Christmas traditions, such as the Christmas tree, come from pagan practices. Wouldn't it be best just to stop celebrating Christmas?

Celebrating the incarnation of Jesus is so meaningful that I think it would be a mistake to stop commemorating it. Whether you have Christmas lights or trees is really irrelevant, as long as we center our celebration on God's gift of His Son.

As for the tree and other practices coming from paganism, this is likely true. At the winter solstice, the Romans celebrated a festival called Saturnalia, in honor of the god of agriculture, Saturnus, by decorating their houses with greens and lights and exchanging gifts. Christians took these practices and gave them a Christian perspective. Although some wonder if this celebration is legitimate, we have a great New Testament lesson to help guide us. In the first century, some believers equated purchasing meat sacrificed to idols from the meat market with engaging in pagan worship. Paul rejected this line of thinking. He wrote, "So then, about eating food sacrificed to idols. . . . food does not bring us near to God; we are no worse if we do not eat, and no better if we do" (1 Cor. 8:4, 8). Eating food offered to an idol is neither right nor wrong; in these neutral areas, we should follow our consciences. It is the same with Christmas paraphernalia, like trees and greens and lights. If you are not engaged in pagan worship and your conscience is free, then enjoy these aspects of the holiday.

That being said, we need to consciously choose to emphasize the incarnation over the commercialization. My wife and I didn't want to eliminate gift giving altogether because we thought it reminded us of God's great gift of the Messiah Jesus for us—"Thanks be to God for his indescribable gift!" (2 Cor. 9:15)—and the gifts the magi brought to the Lord Jesus. But we did choose moderation. We never overwhelmed family members with great quantities or lavishly expensive gifts. And we taught our kids to give to others, especially those more needy than we were.

Another way to keep our focus on Jesus is by including Him in the celebration. As our kids were growing up, we made sure to attend our congregation's worship service as part of our Christmas holiday. On Christmas morning, we read all the biblical narratives related to the Messiah's birth. And although we exchanged gifts, we emphasized that "every good and perfect gift is from above, coming down from the Father of the heavenly lights" (James 1:17), so He is the one for whom we are most thankful.

We also turned Christmas into a celebratory birthday party, with a Happy Birthday banner across our fireplace mantel. My wife made a birthday cake for the Lord, and Christmas was the only morning of the year that our kids were permitted to eat cake for breakfast. December 25 may not actually be Jesus' birthday, but it is as good as any day to celebrate the incarnation of the King.

—*M. R.*

52. If Christ died for all of our sins, past, present, and future, and we have accepted His death on the cross, what does 1 John 1:9 mean about confessing sins so that we will be forgiven?

Christ's redemption of believers secures God's forgiveness of our sins (Eph. 1:7). When Christ died on the cross in our place, as the propitiation for our sins—which means He satisfied the just need for payment as the penalty for sin demanded by a holy God—He took the judgment we deserved because of our sin against God (Rom. 3:23–25). The moment anyone believes the word of truth about Christ's death and resurrection, the believer secures this forgiveness as part of one's salvation (Rom. 10:9–10; Eph. 1:13).

In other words, a person who comes to Christ confesses sin and is forgiven. Forgiveness removes the penalty due our sins, but forgiveness does not stop anyone from sinning. All sin strains the relationship between believers and our Father, and so we seek forgiveness in order to put right our relationship with God. The confession that John speaks of in 1 John 1:9 is the confession of these sins. We are confessing that we have wronged Him with our disobedience, and we affirm that we desire to do what is pleasing to Him. Confession enables us to continue to move forward in our continued fellowship with Him. Salvation is not lost by sin. But sin is something God hates. By confessing sin and seeking forgiveness, we say to God that we hate what He hates and love what He loves—and that we love Him.

—*E. C. R. and M. K.*

53. As we read the Bible, we see *Lord* and *God* used hundreds of times. How do we know what specific name was used in the original Scriptures?

The names *God* and *Lord* found in the English version of the Bible are translations, neither of which were in the original language of the Bible. Scholars suggest that both *Yahweh* and *Jehovah* are two different transcriptions of the Hebrew written name for God. It is usually written as LORD in the English versions of the Bible. The four consonants YHWH represent the ancient Hebrew name for God, and Jews have always considered it too sacred to pronounce. "Thus you shall say to the sons of Israel, 'The LORD, the God of your fathers, the God of Abraham, the God of Isaac, and the God of Jacob, has sent me to you.' This is My name forever, and this is My memorial-name to all generations" (Ex. 3:15 NASB). The name *Adonai* means "Lord," a title used for someone who is a master and worthy of respect and obedience.

One of the most comforting studies we can experience in our devotional time is studying the names of God in the Old Testament and seeing how He reaches out to us in so many ways. He is *Elohim*, "God"; *Jehovah / Yahweh*, "the Self-existent One"; *Jehovah-jireh*, "the Lord will provide." This last was the name Abraham gave to the place where he sacrificed the ram (caught in the thicket on Mount Moriah) in Isaac's place. Abraham needed a substitute for the sacrifice, and God Himself provided it. And through the sacrifice of the Incarnate Son, Jesus Christ, we can have a relationship and fellowship with a Holy God.

God is also *Jehovah-rapha*, "the Lord who heals all of our hurts"; He is called *Jehovah-nissi*, "the Lord our banner." He is the one we can run to, our shelter and our exaltation, and He is *Jehovah-Shalom*, "the Lord our Peace." He is *Jehovah-ra-ah*, "our Shepherd," guarding, guiding, feeding, and correcting. These are only a few of the names of God in Scripture, and further study will reveal even more of His character and how He loves us.

—D. C.

54. Why did Jesus say in Luke 5:32 that He didn't come to preach to the righteous? Did He know that there were some who actually didn't need to repent and so didn't need a Savior for their sins?

Absolutely not. Jesus was not referring at all to *actually* righteous people; He was referring only to those who *thought* that they were better than anyone else. Almost from the very beginning of His ministry, Jesus was attacked by the religious hierarchy: the priests, the Pharisees, and the Sadducees. All of them thought they were above reproach. (Although, when Jesus challenged anyone who was without sin to cast the first stone against the woman caught in adultery, they were miraculously frozen until they crept silently away.)

In this passage, by "righteous," Jesus meant those who were holy in their own sight. Christ was surrounded by sinful people who knew what they were, who knew how they lived, and who knew they needed a Savior. There is only one who is sinless, and His name is Jesus. He came to let the self-righteous know that their lack of honest humility left them open to condemnation as sinners.

—*M. K.*

55. Leviticus 18:21 says that God hates child sacrifice. If that is true, why did He sacrifice His only Son?

The crucifixion of Jesus is very different from child sacrifice. Jesus is God's Son, but He chose to go to the cross. He submitted Himself to do the Father's will. Unlike the pagans who gave up firstborn sons in order to have good weather for their crops, Jesus' death achieved far greater blessings than material gain. The pagans made sacrifices to nonexistent deities or idols; Jesus tasted death so that we could know a relationship and fellowship with a holy God who loves us.

God redeemed sinners with His own blood, through Jesus Christ, His Son. Jesus took the penalty for the sins of the world through His death. Only Jesus, who is both fully God and fully man, could accomplish that. In that sense, the death of Jesus was unlike any other sacrifice. And most importantly, unlike any pagan child sacrifice, God raised Jesus from the dead after three days. The resurrection of Jesus proves that His death was not a hopeless attempt to appease a false idol—His death was an act of faith and obedience that pleased God, who raised Him. The death and resurrection of Jesus made possible the salvation of all humanity.

—*M. K.*

56. I know that God knows all things, but I don't understand why He asks people questions. Could you help me understand why an omniscient God asks people questions?

I am delighted to deal with this question. You are correct in your observation that God is omniscient, i.e., all-knowing. God is infinite and unlimited in knowledge and understanding (Ps. 147:5). From all eternity, the Lord knows all things past, present, and future instantly, truly, and exhaustively (Isa. 46:9–10). There is not one iota of knowledge that God does not possess! He is God!

It is important to note that omniscience is not an attribute that God has acquired through an educational process (Isa. 40:13–14). God is omniscient by nature. By His nature, there is not anything that God does not know, nor is there anything that is hidden from God (Heb. 4:13). What is absolutely stunning is that God, being infinite, knows Himself perfectly (Matt. 11:27; 1 Cor. 2:10–12). Only the infinite can know fully and exhaustively the infinite. The Lord knows perfectly from all eternity everything about you and me, even down to the number of hairs on our head (Ps. 139:1–6; Matt. 10:30).

You are correct in your observation that God asks us questions. In Genesis 3 and 4 God asks nine questions. In Genesis 18 the Lord asks Abraham one of the most memorable questions in Scripture: "Is anything too hard for the Lord?" (v. 14). After washing the disciples' feet in the upper room, the Lord Jesus asks them a penetrating question: "Do you understand what I have done for you?" (John 13:12). The apostle Paul never forgot the question that our glorified Lord posed to him on the Damascus road: "Saul, Saul, why do you persecute me?" (Acts 9:4).

Now since God is omniscient, it is obvious that He does not ask us questions in order to be informed. He does not ask us questions because He does not know what is going on in our lives. He knows everything that is going on in our lives. God asks us questions for our good. God cares for us so much that He asks us questions designed to lead us to face our sin, to think about our choices, to lead us to repentance, and to move us to trust and have confidence in Himself. I thank God for the questions that He asks us in Scripture. I must add that we can learn much about helping one another from the example of God Himself. Instead of telling a person everything we know about their problem, issue, or sin, perhaps a well-crafted question could go a long way in helping that person come to faith in Christ and start to make biblically based choices in life.

—*W. N.*

57. Why doesn't God do something about the pain and suffering in the world?

The question implies the existence of a Being (God) *able* to eliminate pain, if only He were willing. Surely He knows we are often quite miserable. We human beings are so constructed that pain is sometimes unavoidable. Our nerve endings howl in protest when our bodies are injured. And we are not the only creatures who experience pain. Animals suffer too. But our pain may be intensified by our ability to anticipate it and to question it. If God can stop it, why doesn't He?

The answer may be, in part, that God *does* stop it many times. Read the life of Jesus as recorded in the New Testament. On some occasions, He nearly exhausted Himself healing sick people—as God the Father's surrogate. But He did not treat every sick person in the land. He could not have done it without compromising His mission, which was to preach and teach the Word of God and, when the time came, to die for our sins. Time and space made it practically impossible for Him to wipe out sickness and pain during His time on earth.

God in Heaven is not hindered by the limitations imposed on Jesus by the incarnation. He doesn't grow weary or get thirsty or have to ask, "Who touched me?" Yet even God in Heaven cannot do *everything* that we mortals might ask Him to do, including the complete elimination of pain and suffering. It is not strictly correct to say that God can do anything. He *cannot* deny Himself (2 Tim. 2:13 NASB), He *cannot* lie (Titus 1:2), and He *cannot* be tempted by evil (James 1:13). These and similar statements about God imply that His activity in the universe is constrained by the reality of His character.

Another reality is the fall, meaning that Adam's and Eve's initial transgression resulted in a state of alienation from God. Humanity's natural disposition has been bondage to sin ever since. Yet we retain elements of the image of God, including freedom to make choices. With that freedom, we can and often do choose to sin, and sin brings sad consequences, including pain and suffering. God acts in a broken universe where He cannot bless His creatures to the extent that He would if not for their abuse of freedom.

Even so, "The LORD is good to all; he has compassion on all he has made" (Ps. 145:9). Read Psalm 103 for insights into the ways of God that most directly affect us. From many other texts, see how He has planned a pain-free eternity for His redeemed people. In due time, He will make everything conform to His design.

—D. C.

PART TWO

Is it okay for Christians to go on strike?

and other questions about life and living it biblically

58. I have a friend who often prefaces her remarks with the words, "The Lord told me." The Lord tells her many things—to go here or there, to buy or not buy an item, even to give advice to a friend. I have at times been the recipient of that unsolicited advice. How do I think about this and process that kind of spiritual certainty?

You are right to be uneasy about your friend's approach. It is not a good practice for anyone to say the Lord has spoken to him or her about another person's life. Such an approach can be presumptuous and often lacks the foundation of a relationship context necessary for someone to receive such advice. Obviously, there are times when we should be corrected by good friends, especially if our lives are not in order. But even that should be done carefully and compassionately on the basis of scriptural truth, not on the claim to a personal message from God.

This kind of approach—to declare that the Lord has given specific advice for someone else—has the danger of spiritual abuse and manipulation. Furthermore, to liberally say the Lord is directing too many specific details of life is to treat Him like a GPS, when we already have and know the map that provides foundational biblical principles for conducting our lives. And these biblical principles also give us good common sense.

—R. d.

59. I've been a Christian for a long time, and I started out praying a lot, but it just seemed like my prayers weren't being answered. I began to think that maybe only special people get their prayers answered, so I stopped praying. What's wrong with me?

I think part of the problem we have as believers is that we hear verses like John 14:14: "You may ask me for anything in my name, and I will do it," and we think that's like "open, sesame" to anything we want. If you think about it, no wise parent would tell their kids they can have everything . . . including things that are bad for them. A medicine cabinet is a good thing, but my kids knew early on that not everything in there was good for them.

A Christian needs to realize that Jesus' statement is not a blanket statement: it is to be taken within the context of all that the Bible says about prayer. Sometimes we ask for silly things—things that are probably selfish and wrong for us. "When you ask, you do not receive, because you ask with wrong motives, that you may spend what you get on your pleasures" (James 4:3).

When we pray we ought to consider what God thinks about our requests. Is this His will? A good prayer is when we ask God to give us only what He wants and to keep us from that which He doesn't want for us. Some of the best answers I've ever received to my prayers were the ones when God simply said no. When you pray you ought to have faith that God will do what is best in every situation in your life (see James 1:5).

As people of prayer, we ought to be living in a way that pleases God, not necessarily perfect, but certainly with a heart that wants to glorify Him. Prayer warriors live in such a way as to honor God and love people. So I strive always to keep my conscience clear before God and man.

—*M. K.*

60. Is it right to find someone to date online? It seems like many people are doing it, including many Christians. I just don't know how to think about this.

I don't think going to good dating sites is wrong, and I have known people who successfully found husbands and wives that way. The most important thing to consider, however, is your motivation and the way the dating site manages the process. One must know one's theology and one's heart. We are living in a deceptive time, and we can be self-deceived. Does the dating site seem to come from a sound theological premise, asking the important questions about faith and character and authentic interests? Or does it get into trivial, image-based questions and promote sentimental idealism, making claims about all the perfect relationships and promising you the answer to all your dreams—something that God does not guarantee on this earth. Are you using this venue because you think you can know more about a person this way (that can be true) or because you are desperate to find someone?

Elisabeth Elliot quoted her husband, Jim, as saying, "Let not our longing slay the appetite of our living." Having a spouse is a God-implanted longing, but His will and His standard must guide your life and your choices.

—*R. d.*

61. Why should we pay taxes to a government that misuses our money? Some tax receipts are used to fund abortion clinics overseas, and there are other misuses of tax money. Don't we have a moral responsibility to withhold taxes?

Not if you want to stay out of jail. But there are at least two or three other reasons for paying taxes cheerfully. First, note the example of Jesus. After asserting that He was personally exempt, He told Peter to pay the requested tax anyway, "so that we may not cause offense" (Matt. 17:27). We can be reasonably sure that the Roman government used Jesus' tax money for many unsavory purposes. A second reason is that good government institutions depend on tax revenue for their existence. Taxes are used to fund police and fire departments and—in order to provide protection—armies and navies and air forces. Study Romans 13:1–7.

A third reason for paying taxes is "quality of life" benefits received in exchange for them. These include safe water supplies, paved highway systems, street lights, parks, public health departments, and so on. To experience a society with very few taxes, move to a majority-world country where governments collect little and return even less.

—*D. C.*

62. A dear friend of mine went to be with the Lord recently, and when I attended the memorial service I learned that my friend's body was going to be cremated. I had always thought that cremation was pagan, but it seems that more and more believers opt for cremation over burial. What does God's Word say?

Nothing. That is, it doesn't touch on the propriety of cremation. Every instance referring to the death of a believer is followed by traditional burial. But there is no injunction against cremation. In some countries there is not enough land to allow for cemeteries. Many people are not buried in the ground; many sailors, for example, have been buried at sea. Some arrogant people deny the resurrection and call for cremation as a way of preventing it. They're a little naïve, I'd say. If God created man (Adam) originally from the dust of the earth, I'm sure He'd have absolutely no trouble putting any body together after the resurrection. After all, He's the Creator.

The thing to concentrate on as a child of God is that the body we live in now is temporary. Scripture says, we are "absent from the body and . . . at home with the Lord" when we die (2 Cor. 5:8 NASB). When I told a man selling burial plots that I was planning on cremation after I leave this old world, he said in a manipulative way, "Do you have any idea how hot that crematorium is when a body burns?" I said, "No, and I don't care. I won't be in that outer shell any more." As 2 Corinthians 4:18 says, "We fix our eyes not on what is seen, but on what is unseen, since what is seen is temporary but what is unseen is eternal." And that includes our eternal bodies.

—*M. K.*

63. Is it okay for Christians to give their bodies to the needs of science?

People donate their bodies to science so that medical schools can use them for study, the idea being that poking and cutting a real body gives medical students a better understanding of physiology and anatomy than when working only with books and drawings. The question here implies that collaborating with medical schools or science labs may not be a congenial Christian activity.

Two considerations help us deal with the issue. The first is a fact of universal acceptance, the second a Christian belief. The first fact is that death, which befalls everybody, is irreversible and something must be done with dead bodies. The process is the same for everybody; all that is different is the rate of decay, which is determined by the condition of the body at the time of death or things done to it after death, such as embalmment. Everybody knows this, and everybody treats a dead body in more or less the same way: embalm and bury it, or cremate it and scatter the ashes.

The second consideration is a powerful Christian truth: our bodies are the subject of redemption and therefore will be raised from the dead. This affects the way Christians cope with death, including acceptance of the fact of death and treatment of the body "abandoned" temporarily by its former tenant.

We Christians grieve, but not hysterically and not callously, as if getting rid of the body were a funeral's primarily goal. We have respect for the body, and we strive to show respect for it, whether by burial or by cremation. We do not just sling it into a pit and shovel dirt over it; this means that if giving a dead body to science is judged to be compatible with respect for the now irreversibly decaying remains, there can be no objection to it.

—D. C.

64. When I reprimand a relative for moral sin, he replies, "Jesus said, 'Judge not!' So stop picking on me." How can I explain that it is right to judge some things?

In Matthew 18:15–20, Jesus tells the disciples what to do when a brother or sister sins against them. The first step is to "point out their fault."

The apostle Paul taught the church in Corinth that it was their responsibility to judge a member who was committing flagrant sin. "Expel the wicked person from among you," he commanded (1 Cor. 5:12–13; see also Titus 3:10).

The words, "Do not judge," are part of a paragraph about hypocrisy (Matt. 7:1–5). Jesus rebuked His listeners for being upset about a "speck of sawdust" in another person's eye while ignoring the "plank" in their own. His language was figurative; the speck of sawdust stands for a relatively insignificant fault. A plank, on the other hand, is something much more serious. A person who is guilty of serious sin is in no position to correct anyone else. Not until he has gotten rid of the plank is he qualified to "remove the speck" from his brother's eye.

Note that Jesus implies that for someone who had removed the plank in his own eye, it would be okay to remove the speck in somebody else's eye. Thus, His admonition not to judge was not a flat prohibition against judging.

Romans 14, especially verses 12 and 13, add another dimension to the subject. The chapter stresses several truths: first, sometimes believers disagree about the meaning and application of biblical issues. Second, we must answer to God for our respective views, not to those whose interpretation may differ from ours. Third, for two reasons God alone is qualified to judge us: first, we are His servants, and second, He alone knows our hearts. "Who are [we] to judge someone else's servant?" Paul asks. He might add, who are we to think we know someone else's motives?

In light of material in the Epistles, we interpret the warning not to judge as, "Do not judge another person's motives. That person answers to God, not to you, and God alone knows what is in the heart. But do not overlook conduct that is clearly sinful. Deal with it."

—D. C.

65. Some of my relatives are "gospel hardened." They have heard the gospel all their lives but sneer at it. Do I have to go on praying for them? I don't feel like it.

Some Christians think that praying endlessly for people who show no sign of repentance and belief is like casting pearls before swine. But that expression may be more applicable to preaching or evangelizing than to prayer (Matt. 7:6). Don't wear your tongue out preaching to your willfully hardened loved one—but prayer is something else. The text warning us not to cast pearls before swine is followed by an exhortation to pray (see vv. 7–10).

The apostle Paul said that his heart's desire and prayer to God was that others might be saved (Rom. 10:1). Maybe he was encouraged to do so by his own inspired words in 1 Timothy 2:3–8, and by Peter's words in 2 Peter 3:9. Look them up and read them.

—D. C.

66. I am having trouble with Paul's words "forgetting what is behind" (Phil. 3:13). How can we just simply forget the past?

I agree with you—we are not computers! We can't just press the delete button and remove files of life from our memory banks. Some of us truly wish we did have the capacity to erase sinful, sorrowful, and painful memories from our minds and dreams. And despite our best efforts to forget, sometimes an unwanted memory as real as our breath this morning invades our minds. Sometimes we try to suppress memories in unhealthy ways.

However, in the biblical sense, *forgetting* does not mean deleting or suppressing the memories of the past. Forgetting in the biblical sense is also not the passive notion of forgetting; for example, you may have every intention to call someone but then have a memory lapse from being caught up in the busyness of the day.

Biblical *forgetting* is a choice. We do not delete or suppress the past but face it. In the power of the Holy Spirit, we choose not to allow the failures, hurt, pain, and sins of the past to hinder or prevent us in our walk with God in the present. We do not allow the victories of the past to make us complacent in the present, nor do we allow the pain and failures of the past to paralyze us in the present. It is important to note that the word *forgetting* is in the present tense. Choosing not to be bound by the past is an ongoing discipline of Christian living.

—W. N.

67. Ever since I found a Moody Radio station, going to church has been difficult for me. The pastor can't preach like the radio preachers. He is alternately boring and irritating. Is it okay for me to stay home and listen to the radio?

No, it is not okay. Hearing preaching on the radio can be very beneficial, and we can learn a great deal, but radio programs (or online services) that are broadcast during church hours on Sunday are for the benefit of shut-ins and others who cannot go to church. For the rest of us, church attendance is critically important. Acts 2:46 reports that the members of the first church in Jerusalem "continued to meet together." Some time later, believers were exhorted to not give up "meeting together, as some are in the habit of doing, but encouraging one another—and all the more as you see the Day approaching" (Heb. 10:25).

We go to church for several reasons, one of which is to encourage each other. We need each other. We ought to go to church with the prayer that we might be used by God to encourage a disconsolate brother or sister. As for boring preachers, I suppose I myself am one on occasion. But I make myself boredom-proof when someone else is preaching by resolving to listen to the speaker. You'd be surprised how interesting an ordinary preacher can be if you really listen to what he has to say.

—*D. C.*

68. I heard there is a biblical reference regarding tattoos. Many of my unsaved relatives have gotten them and I want to point out God's view on the subject.

The Hebrew word translated tattoo appears only in Leviticus 19:28, where it is linked with "cuttings" (mutilations) in the body to honor the dead. Cuttings and tattoos alike were prohibited. They were pagan practices.

Tattooing should be distinguished from "marks" intended to express intense loyalty to the Lord. Check these in Deuteronomy 6:8; 11:18; 14:1; Isaiah 44:5; and 49:16, where the Lord says to His people, "I have engraved you on the palms of my hands."

In modern America, tattooing is not sacral, as it was in ancient times. People sometimes get tattooed to identify themselves as members of a group, or they think they are "making a statement." It is a matter of personal judgment whether or not you feel that a tattoo is appropriate. As for your relatives, it's more important to share God's love with them than to scold them for a tattoo choice they have made.

—*D. C.*

69. Why do I find it so difficult to pray? I want to begin my day with God, but when I wake up, I feel like there's too much to do to make prayer practical.

You, of course, are not alone. First, you have a body that doesn't want to get out of bed, an agenda that prompts you to put it off until you can find more time at the end of the day, and that nagging feeling that maybe prayers don't change a thing, anyway. It's that ongoing battle that we fight against the world, the flesh, and the devil (Eph. 6:12; 1 John 2:16). In the garden of Eden, Adam knew what it meant to seek a conversation with God, to seek to know what He wants, and to desire to do what He wants. Since Adam and Eve fell into sin, the relationship with God has been fractured, and we find talking with God, reading the Word, and obeying it can be just plain hard work. We are fighting against our own sin nature continuously (Rom. 7:18–20).

The best answer to this problem is, to paraphrase the sneaker company, just do it. Wake up in the morning, and before you even get out of bed, offer a simple greeting to God: "Good morning, God. I love You, God, and I know You love me too. God, what are You up to? Whatever it is, I want to be a part of it this morning."

We think prayer has to be long, formal conversations. Instead it can be simple sentences offered throughout the day, giving God praise, making a confession, sharing our needs, or offering Him thanksgiving. When prayer becomes real like this, it becomes as vital to our lives as breathing. We discover it's not a chore or burden, it's the sweetest time in our day.

"Good morning, God. I love You, God, and I know You love me, too."

—*M. K.*

70. I am a teenager. Do I have to attend my parents' church? It is awfully dull. The music is like songs done at funerals, and the preacher is older than my grandfather. I want to go to a real church.

I usually advise teenagers to go to church with their parents, in that way exhibiting suitable submission to them. That is one way to honor them (Eph. 6:2). Additionally, it nourishes family solidarity and teaches you to exist without constant entertainment, whether in school or in church. And, it secures for you the respect given by older folk to teens who show a little humility. Some of your peers reject discipline and a time of subordination, as if they, the teens, knew more than their parents and other "fossils." In time, if they acquire wisdom, they are then ashamed of their attitude during their teen years.

However, I understand your discontent. You need the fellowship of sprightly believers in a lively church. The answer may be to become part of two groups, until such a time when it is no longer necessary to support your parents in their church. Perhaps you could find another youth group or Bible study to attend in addition to supporting your parents at their church. Eventually, if you conduct yourself with decorum, you may persuade your parents that they also ought to be connected to a group of people "on fire for God," as the expression goes.

—*D. C.*

71. What is fellowship? I am a new Christian, and I hear this word a lot.

The term is frequently used loosely to indicate pious socializing. It is derived from a Greek word (*koinonia*) that is translated "fellowship" fifteen times in the King James Version and twelve times in the NIV translation of the Bible. In other places, the same word is rendered "participation" (1 Cor. 10:16), a "partnership" (Philem. 6), and in the KJV, "communion," where most recent translations prefer "sharing" or "partnership" (Phil. 1:5).

We share a common life in Christ, and therefore, we are partners in the truth, sharing the love and warmth that we have as Christians. True fellowship is infinitely richer than mere socializing, though it surely includes socializing.

—D. C.

72. Is trouble that comes into our lives a sign of punishment from God?

I believe that the Bible does not teach that all trouble is a sign of punishment. As a matter of fact, Jesus said, "In this world you will have trouble. But take heart! I have overcome the world" (John 16:33). When trouble does come our way, it's good to examine our lives to see if there is an offense against God in our lives (see Ps. 139:24). While God often chastens those He loves, it certainly is not punishment, but He disciplines us as a way of changing our conduct (see John 15:2). God warned Israel many times that their conduct was an embarrassment to

Him before the other nations, and they would be punished. Israel's exile to Babylon was an example of a horrific judgment on God's chosen people.

Scripture gives us other examples of trouble and suffering, however. Job was a righteous, faithful man who experienced tremendous, heartbreaking trouble. In the book of Acts, the disciples suffered greatly because they were faithful to Christ. After being flogged for testifying about Jesus, "the apostles left the Sanhedrin, rejoicing because they had been counted worthy of suffering disgrace for the Name" (Acts 5:41). Clearly this trouble was not a punishment from God! It will take wisdom and sensitivity to the conviction of the Holy Spirit for us to know the difference between His discipline in our lives and other reasons why we experience sorrow and trials.

—*M. K.*

73. At my job and in my living situation, many of my colleagues and neighbors are living secular, even alternative, lifestyles. They joke about the specifics of their lives casually, even graphically, and at times they put down things that are sacred to me. Sometimes I am confused about how to handle conversations and jokes in a Christian way without sounding self-righteous. How do I respond so they know I am not condoning their lifestyles and ideas but am still approachable? My tendency has probably been to stay quiet or to make too many concessions.

This is a good question, one that I think many of us wonder about in a world that has lost its moral compass and is becoming increasingly hostile and at times even litigious about expressed Christian values and teaching. In conversation about this issue, a friend once said to me that the best response is a sober one. I love the word sober; its definitions include "habitually temperate" and "quiet or sedate." Romans 12:3 tells the Christian to "think soberly," or, as one translation puts it, "think of yourself with sober judgment." In the context of that passage, Christians are exhorted not to think of themselves as better than other Christians. The principle is true consistently with anyone, believer or unbeliever: we are to think of ourselves in a way that points our conduct toward sobriety, humility, wisdom, and discretion. The opposite of that would be thinking that leads to pride, out of which comes foolish behavior.

In the case you are asking about, examples of foolish behavior would include throwing truth at those who don't believe or joining too casually in inappropriate jesting and behavior. Second Corinthians 6:14 asks us to consider the rhetorical questions: "What do righteousness and wickedness have in common? Or what fellowship can light have with darkness?" The implied answer is "none." Soberness, then, becomes a way to think about our posture in situations where we cannot join in—not an attitude of dour disapproval but the distance of polite seriousness. Finally, the respect with which we treat those around us may in time earn us the ability to give our perspective on what matters in life.

—R. d.

74. In my view, the Lord's solution to the problem of heart adultery in Matthew 5:27–30 is extreme. How am I to understand our Lord's words? Is He saying that we are literally to gouge out our eyes and cut off our right hand in order to deal with the problem of the sinful desires of our hearts?

Our Lord's language of gouging out the right eye and cutting off the right hand is shocking. In fact, New Testament scholar D. A. Carson suggests that right hand may be a euphemism for the male sex organ, making the language even more graphic. Some have taken His words to mean just that. For example, centuries ago, Origen, a leader in the ancient church, was so disturbed by his own inner lusts that he is said to have had himself castrated.

But literally gouging out an eye or cutting off a hand cannot solve the lust problems of the heart (see Col. 2:20–23). In this passage Jesus is using a figure of speech called hyperbole, a deliberate overstatement of the truth, to emphasize to us how serious the issue is. The sense of desperation, visceral physical reactions, and horror we feel and experience in imagining the literal maiming in response to lust is exactly how we ought to feel and think about our impure imaginations. We should have a holy, godly, and Spirit-empowered sense of desperation about getting sin out our lives, a complete conviction about maintaining the sanctification and purity of our hearts and our imaginations. Jesus uses overstatement to emphasize the importance of the exclusive devotion between a husband and wife in action, heart, mind, and the deepest recesses of imagination.

—*W. N.*

75. How far should a Christian go with political involvement? Some people say that this world is not our home and that we should just trust the Lord, looking ahead to what God has promised us eternally. Others seem to feel there is a place for Christians to protest against practices that contradict what the Bible clearly teaches, such as abortion.

As Christians we must search our hearts to know what each one of us is called to do and in what way. We were placed in this world to be witnesses for Christ in word and action. The idea of looking ahead to eternity does not avoid the difficulties of cultural life on earth. Living unaware, insular lives is never an option. We cannot keep our service and outreach within comfortable venues. Any action, however, must be solidly based on scriptural truth and done for love of that truth. For example, the genocide of the unborn taking place on a regular basis in this country grieves God and should grieve us. Psalm 127:3 says, "Children are a heritage from the LORD, offspring a reward from him." And Proverbs 6:16–17 notes, "The LORD hates . . . hands that shed innocent blood." To deliberately end the life of an unborn baby is murder. Trying to persuade those who are contemplating abortion to choose otherwise and taking steps to show the horror of abortive practices—these are courageous acts when done with humility. Our desire should be both to protest against a societal evil and to protect life.

Protecting life could also include supporting organizations like crisis pregnancy centers, which work not only to educate but also to care emotionally and practically for women who may think they have no other option than abortion. In these times, we have to take a good look at the courage that being a Christian demands, the kind of courage that is willing to pay a price.

—*R. d.*

76. Why is it that we keep reading about ministers, priests, and other highly visible religious leaders being caught in sin?

While it saddens us as evangelicals to see these repugnant headlines about people who have in some public way misrepresented the name of Christ, clearly their failures are fodder for the media. It's obvious that some readers and listeners want to read and hear this stuff. (I've often wondered if the media holds itself to the same standards of conduct as they do clergy, but that's another topic.)

The world often doesn't understand that in order to be a member of the body of Christ, you must admit that you're a sinner and need a Savior. There's only one who can save, and His name is Jesus Christ. Becoming an authentic Christian doesn't mean that you'll never sin again. As a matter of fact, 1 John 1:8 says, "If we claim to be without sin, we deceive ourselves and the truth is not in us." What truth is that? The truth of the gospel. The passage goes on to say, "If we confess our sins, he [God] is faithful and just and will forgive us our sins and to purify us from all unrighteousness" (1 John 1:9).

The truth is that the vast majority of ministers are being faithful to God daily and are not being caught up in the vile things of this world. But if they sin they have an Advocate with the Father, Jesus Christ, just as does every other person who calls out to God for forgiveness.

Most of the pastors and Christian leaders I know are being faithful to their calling. They're not hypocrites involved in immoral things. The vast majority of them want to finish well, walking circumspectly in this world. We need to pray for our pastors and leaders. They face the same temptations that all of us do. They need the encouragement of our prayers for them.

All of us as believers, when we hear of notable people falling into sin, should be reminded that we are to keep short accounts with God ourselves. We should also seek to surround ourselves with people who love us and will hold us accountable.

—*M. K.*

77. I have an atheist friend who believes that selfless acts of kindness can be explained by the evolutionary process. But that seems counterintuitive. Can you help me out?

This is a common response offered by atheists who want to provide some kind of naturalistic grounding for altruistic acts. Both the Christian and the atheist affirm the existence of selfless acts of kindness. Peter Singer wants Americans to give up Starbucks coffee and bottled water in order to feed the hungry children of the world. This is noble. But as an ardent atheist, how does Singer, and others like him, frame these suggestions so that they are not the mere opinion of an individual but an imperative with a moral force? If it is merely a suggestion, then it would be nice if Americans endured personal sacrifice for the needs of the world.

But if it is a moral imperative, then there is a sense of "oughtness" that should leave the comfortable uncomfortable.

Many atheists turn to biological altruism as their source. We often hear stories of vampire bats who will regurgitate blood and donate it to members of their group who failed to feed that night, or individual Vervet monkeys who signal alarm at the presence of a prey to enhance the survival of the rest of the group while decreasing their own chances. Atheists say that such altruistic behavior is built into our genetic past. Members of a species will sacrifice their personal well-being to increase the survival of those who share their genes, as in a parent for a child (kinship altruism). Interspecies altruism is also found when there is mutual benefit (reciprocal altruism).

There is a problem, however. Both of these categories are ultimately selfish in nature. A cost/benefit analysis forms the basis for judging the worth of these actions (whether consciously or not). But the kind of selfless kindness that we deem moral functions in the reverse. The less benefit received, the more praiseworthy the act. Sacrificing your life for your child is one thing; for your enemy—that's a whole new story.

Something or some event must transform biological altruism with its selfish aims into a moral altruism that is selfless. Atheist proponents of this view point to the rise of consciousness in our evolutionary history. A conscious, thinking being can choose to perform altruistic acts without considering the ultimate benefits to one's self or to those who are close. But as soon as one proposes such an event, we are back to the original question. What is the basis by which a conscious being can proclaim a selfless kind of altruism as being morally superior to a biological form of altruism? Ultimately, evolutionary theories alone cannot explain human capacity for selfless acts of kindness.

—*D. R.*

78. What does it mean to be a spiritual person as described in 1 Corinthians 2:15?

Found on many postmodern lips today are the words: "I am not religious, but I am a spiritual person." If a person attends church on a regular basis, some people consider that to qualify as being a spiritual person. Others assert that being spiritual is in vogue, exhorting people to reject religion in favor of "taking care of your spirit." In light of postmodern culture's concern for the spirit and interest in spirituality, your question is pertinent.

In the Bible, the word "*spiritual*" is not a mood or a cultural trend. In the Scripture, it means belonging to, corresponding to, or caused by God the Holy Spirit (Rom. 1:11; 7:14; 15:27; 1 Cor. 10:3; 12:1–11; Eph. 1:3; 5:19; 1 Peter 2:5). The only instance where this is not the case is in Ephesians 6:12, where one of the descriptions of our demonic enemies is "spiritual forces of evil."

In 1 Corinthians 2:15, the spiritual person is a born-again Christian who lives his or her life in the power and energy of God the Holy Spirit. Such believers yield their lives to the Lord, consistently saying no to the flesh and its sinful desires, and yes to the Holy Spirit (Rom. 6:12–14). Through yielding their lives to the Spirit by faith, the power of the Spirit is unleashed in them, and He enables them to live a life that pleases God (Gal. 5:16–17). The Holy Spirit controls their attitudes, words, and behavior, and empowers their witness.

They demonstrate the supernatural fruit of the Spirit in their character (Gal. 5:22–25). Much more could be said here, but it is enough to say that it is God's will for every follower of Christ to be filled or controlled by the Spirit (Eph. 5:18). Remember, even believers who consistently walk in the power of the Spirit have not arrived at perfection in their spiritual journey, and every stage of life brings with it new challenges that require practical sanctification and fresh power from the Spirit.

79. Candidates for political office make so many conflicting promises, it's hard to know what to believe. What are we as Christians to do?

The words of the apostle Paul are as relevant for our situation today as at the time he wrote them under the inspiration of the Holy Spirit: "I urge, then, first of all, that petitions, prayers, intercession and thanksgiving be made for all people—for kings and all those in authority, that we may live peaceful and quiet lives in all godliness and holiness" (1 Tim. 2:1–2). Though we might feel confused or dismayed by the promises of political leaders, the Lord remains in control (see Prov. 21:1; Rom. 13:1–7). What God desires from Christians during an election season are our prayers and our commitment to holy lives that please Him. No matter who wins an election, our confidence in God should remain firm, knowing that He is the ruler of the universe and the Lord of our lives.

—*M. K.*

80. Nothing I do seems even close to pleasing my wife, who nags me constantly. Frankly, I'm fed up. The single life sure looks appealing these days. Marriage is just too much work. What can I do to change her?

A lot of us men seem to think that it's the woman's responsibility to make a marriage work. While I believe that it takes two to make a marriage work, I think ultimately it's the husband's responsibility to show love to his wife. It's his responsibility to make a marriage work. Colossians 3:19 says, "Husbands, love your wives and do not be harsh with them." Philippians 2:3 exhorts believers: "Do nothing out of selfish ambition or vain conceit. Rather, in humility value others above yourselves." While it's true that these verses are written to us all, I think they have special application to husbands. We need to try to put ourselves into the place where we strive to see things from the wife's perspective.

The problem with most of us as husbands is that we're entirely too egocentric (the root of all sin, by the way) and think that the rules of marriage revolve around us. We should be men who make every effort to love our wives in such a way as to allow them to respect us. We should be our wives' best cheerleaders. Is it work? You bet it is. Is it worth it? Oh, yes.

—*M. K.*

81. Is it true that as long as a person is sincere in his belief, God will admit him or her to Heaven?

No, it is not true. Faith, not sincerity, is the means of salvation. Furthermore, faith has to be properly directed: it must be faith in Jesus Christ. Faith (or belief) in the wrong medicine might kill you. In the same way, belief in a witchdoctor or Buddhist priest or any other system of religion will not save you; it will lead you to Hell.

It's crucial to understand that all of us are guilty before God. We need a Savior, and the only Savior who can save is Jesus Christ, God's own Son. His voluntary death on our behalf makes it morally possible for God to forgive us without compromising His holiness. God does not sweep our sins under the rug; He laid them on Jesus.

However, forgiveness and salvation are not automatic. We also have a part to play. Our part is to respond to God in faith. That's one way of saying that we must open our hearts to the Lord and believe; we must receive Jesus as the Savior.

—*D. C.*

82. Do you have to forgive yourself in order for God to forgive you?

No. That being said, some observations about forgiveness are in order. First, the moment a person receives Christ as their personal Lord and Savior, God grants that person the forgiveness of all their sins—sins past, sins present, and sins future (Eph. 1:7; Heb. 10:17–18). Some Christians call this judicial forgiveness because it deals with God as judge and is related to salvation.

Second, if a Christian sins, it is not a matter of salvation, but it is a matter of fellowship with the Father. Sin does not cause Christians to lose their salvation, but sin does break their fellowship with the heavenly Father. In order for fellowship to be restored, we must confess our sins. One benefit that we will have as a result of confession is forgiveness (1 John 1:9–2:12). We call this paternal forgiveness because it does not deal with our relationship with God as judge but with our fellowship with God as our Father. When people sin against us and ask for forgiveness, it is our biblical responsibility to extend forgiveness to them (Eph. 4:32; Col. 3:13). When we refuse to extend forgiveness to those who ask for it, our refusal is sin and consequently interrupts our fellowship with God and constitutes an obstacle to our reception of God's paternal forgiveness (Matt. 18:21–35).

Third, guilt plagues some Christians, and the ugly memory of their own sins and moral failures haunts them. They cannot find relief even though they know theoretically that the Lord has forgiven them. In order to help such believers cope with their guilt, some concerned believers advise them to forgive themselves so that they can experience liberty and freedom. Here, the pastoral agenda is commendable, but the theology is problematic. We are not told anywhere in the Scripture to forgive ourselves in order to experience God's forgiveness. What we have to do is take our stand on what God says in His Word. When God the Father declares that He has forgiven us, that fact alone should comfort our troubled souls and relieve our guilty conscience. Rest in God's gracious Word and rejoice in the forgiveness that He grants to you!

—W. N.

83. Can a Christian lose his or her salvation?

This is a question that must be answered carefully. A person who knows Christ as personal Lord and Savior, is washed in the blood of Jesus, and is born of the Spirit of God can never be lost! The Lord Jesus Himself asserts:

"My sheep listen to my voice; I know them, and they follow me. I give them eternal life, and *they shall never perish*; no one will snatch them out of my hand. My Father, who has given them to me, is greater than all; no one can snatch them out of my Father's hand. I and the Father are one" (John 10:27–30, italics added).

The Lord Jesus declares in the strongest language possible that *His* sheep will never perish. The words *shall never* are the translation of the strongest negation in the Greek language. In other words, the Lord says *My* sheep will never under any circumstances perish. However, Scripture also indicates that a person who is truly born again will continue in the faith. In fact, continuance or perseverance in the faith is proof and evidence that one knows Christ (John 8:31–32; Col. 1:21–23; Heb. 3:6, 14). While a born-again person cannot be lost, his or her steadfast following of Jesus will be proof of belonging to Christ. This truth serves as a warning to the indifferent or to those who cheapen the grace of God.

—W. N.

84. Lately I've been seeing people in church texting during the service, even when Scripture is read and during prayer. Or they step out to answer a call. I have never heard a minister address this, but it seems wrong.

Such increasing disregard for sacred space and for a service devoted to honoring God should be troubling. Also troubling is the increasing inability for people to be attentive, a basic posture necessary to learning, not to mention for worshiping intelligently. Even movie theaters, recognizing the importance of respect for others, demand that cellphones be turned off, declaring that the offender will be asked to leave if he or she violates that rule. Good symphony halls and opera houses would never tolerate such behavior. How ironic it is that so little prophetic voice is heard in the church, the place where we should regard not only others but also—and more crucially—God.

In an intelligent book, *Still Bored in a Culture of Entertainment*, Richard Winter argues that our culture is at war with and infected by "an epidemic of boredom" because of overstimulation from many sources. One pastor on a blog contends, "The problem is sin. Sin is what insists that nothing is more important than what we are thinking, feeling, desiring, or doing at the moment. Not even God is cause enough for us to turn away from self and quiet our hearts and minds and lips so busy with stuff." Each one of us must consider today's cultural icons and make sure we have thought theologically and biblically about their use.

—*R. d.*

107

85. Who decides what is not okay? I am not thinking about things that are clearly wrong, but things in the gray area. Does public opinion help in accepting or rejecting disputed opinions or conduct?

First, those to whom we turn for guidance in matters of right and wrong should be men and women like Noah, a preacher of righteousness. Because they are in touch with God, they recognize evil when they see it or hear it.

Public opinion can help; it is a factor in deciding whether certain actions or opinions are considered acceptable. But for two reasons, it is risky to lean heavily on public opinion. First, it isn't always easy to determine what the public really believes. Do we depend on polls, and if so, which polls?

Second, public opinion is sometimes seriously wrong. In America's past, slavery was upheld by society at large and even some churches. Women were denied the right to vote, and most men thought that was just dandy. Now, society is steadily yielding ground to those who support moral abominations, such as euthanasia and same-sex marriages. Favoring positions such as these is the fruit of a godless way of thinking.

So where do we turn for guidance? To the Bible, of course. It is what it claims to be: the Word of God. Whom do we believe? In moral matters, we stick with those whose convictions are shaped by the Bible. We discover what convictions people hold by listening to them or reading what they write, and then we compare what these people say with what we are reading in Scripture. Thinking Christians do not accept majority opinions that conflict with what the Bible teaches.

—D. C.

86. Do some babies or small children go to Hell? I hear people say they were saved at age five or six, or even younger. Do you believe kids as young as five get saved? Do they really understand the gospel?

First, there are no babies or small children in Hell. Hell was made for the devil and his angels. They will be joined in that dread place by those who reject Christ and by those who are described in passages such as Matthew 25:41–46, Romans 1–2, and Revelation 21:8. None of these texts have infants or children in view.

In Matthew 18:6, Jesus speaks of "these little ones—those who believe in me." The text does not say that every child believes in Him. But some certainly do.

It is true, of course, that small children do not understand the Trinity or the hypostatic union, etc., but neither do many adult believers. Whether young or old, if you "declare with your mouth, 'Jesus is Lord,' and believe in your heart that God raised him from the dead, you will be saved" (Rom. 10:9). Scripture does not set a certain age as a marker of individual responsibility to respond to the gospel. But the Bible does say that "Everyone who calls on the name of the Lord will be saved" (Rom. 10:13).

If a young child makes a profession of faith, the godly adults in his or her life should nurture that profession through instruction in the Word of God and encouragement in righteous living.

In my judgment, kids who believe in Jesus are truly born again but should reaffirm their faith in Him when they are older.

The new birth is as valid in a child as in an adult, but in most cases an adult more fully understands the implications of the experience. You don't get saved twice, but you should taste afresh the experience of coming to Jesus in faith. You should make a commitment when older to believe in Christ and to serve Him.

—*D. C.*

87. I was baptized in a Baptist church when I was ten years old, but I didn't really I know what it meant. Now a friend in another denomination tells me that my baptism was wrong and that I am not saved. He thinks I need to listen to Peter's first sermon and be re-baptized "in the name of Jesus Christ for the forgiveness of [my] sins" (Acts 2:38). What do you think about this?

In Peter's next encounter with a crowd in Jerusalem, he says simply, "Repent, then, and turn to God, so that your sins may be wiped out" (Acts 3:19). Not a word about baptism. But many Christians engage in fierce debates about the meaning of baptism. An outsider, listening to them, might conclude either that baptism is not terribly important or that salvation is contingent on baptism. These are extreme views, neither of which is correct. Those who hold the second opinion add that the candidate must realize that baptism is "for forgiveness," and that a correct baptismal formula must be observed, such as "in the name of Jesus Christ."

Jesus commanded the apostles to baptize their converts, and they obeyed, as is clear in Acts. Baptism is not an option for

Christians. But their sermons emphasized repentance and faith as the essentials for salvation. Furthermore, in no place in Acts, where the sermons are recorded, is baptism explained. For that matter, the subject is not expounded thoroughly anywhere in the New Testament. Typical of its treatment is Romans 6:1–7. The focus in that paragraph is Christian conduct. Paul says in effect that an easygoing attitude toward sin is unthinkable, given our union with Christ. Baptism portrays that union and is presented in Romans 6 to drive home the point that the doctrine of justification by faith is not an excuse for misbehavior.

As for not understanding the meaning of baptism when you were baptized, take comfort in contemplating the case of Apollos (Acts 18:24–26). He was a powerful preacher when as yet he knew nothing about Christian baptism. Most of us who were baptized as children or in our early teens knew only that Christ had commanded it.

—D. C.

88. A friend owes me money for a professional service but refuses to pay. She says I overcharged her. What should I do? Call her boss and embarrass her until she pays up?

Write it off. To people experiencing similar injustices the apostle Paul said, "Why not rather be wronged? Why not rather be cheated?" (1 Cor. 6:7). It would be better to be cheated than to run the risk of doing wrong yourself. The Lord can easily make up the piddling amount you lose.

—D. C.

89. Is it proper for unbelievers to receive Communion?

In 1 Corinthians 11:23–33, we have clear instructions about how we should participate in the Lord's Supper (also called Communion, the Breaking of Bread, and the Eucharist). The Lord Jesus commands us to break the bread (vv. 23–24) and to drink the cup in remembrance of Him (v. 25). The verbs "do" in verses 24 and 25 are the present imperative tense in Greek, and they could be translated "keep on doing this" in remembrance of Me. The church is commanded to continue the act of the Lord's Supper until Jesus comes again.

The commands themselves are warm and affectionate. When the local church celebrates the Lord's Supper, they collectively proclaim the Lord's death to the world until Christ's return (v. 26). The ongoing proclamation of Christ's death through the public observance of Communion serves as an acted sermon, a witness to the world. The Lord never commands unbelievers to participate in the Lord's Supper. In fact, scriptural evidence supports the following position: communion is only for the reverent and thoughtful participation of believers (vv. 27–32).

—*W. N.*

90. What should we do about the presence of unbelievers in church meetings when Christians celebrate the Lord's Supper?

First, we should thank God that unbelievers are present. Second, we need to be sensitive and careful to reflect Christ's heart for the lost. Third, before the distribution of the elements, I suggest that the pastor, or someone who has skill in the public reading of Scripture, read 1 Corinthians 11:23–31. Such a reading will benefit Christians and unbelievers alike.

Finally, as we explain the biblical parameters of participation, why not extend an invitation to unbelievers to trust Jesus as Lord and Savior? If they trust the Lord, then invite them to join us as a part of God's family and participate with us. Still, even if an unbeliever does participate in the Lord's Supper, the Lord may use their very participation to convict them of sin and bring them to Himself. The Puritan preacher and pastor Solomon Stoddard, who was the grandfather and pastoral mentor of Jonathan Edwards, converted to Christ while he was receiving communion. We can trust that God will assess the hearts of all who are present, and His Spirit will bring conviction, judgment, and salvation as He wills.

—W. N.

91. Every time I wear slacks, which is nearly every day, my mother says I'm being sinful, and she reminds me that the Bible tells women not to wear men's clothing. Is she right?

Your mother is half right; the Bible does tell women not to wear men's clothing. See Deuteronomy 22:5: "A woman must not wear men's clothing, nor a man wear women's clothing, for the LORD your God detests anyone who does this." But her understanding of that text is misguided. Scripture does not define men's clothing, and obviously the notion of appropriate clothing for men and women is different across time and across cultures. Neither men nor women wear the same thing in twenty-first-century America that they did when the Israelites prepared to enter Canaan, when this passage was originally written. The passage is aimed at transvestites, also called "cross-dressers"—men or women who get erotic pleasure from wearing clothing belonging to the opposite sex.

Your mother seems not to believe that slacks or pants are now an acceptable part of a decent woman's wardrobe. She thinks, mistakenly, that pants are still exclusively men's clothing, as they were one hundred years ago. Be assured, she will not even begin to change her mind unless you wear modest pants or jeans. Many Christian women need to heed the apostle Paul's words about their dress styles whether they choose dresses or pants: "I also want the women to dress modestly, with decency and propriety" (1 Tim. 2:9).

—D. C.

92. What do you do when a person who is causing conflict will not confess, continues to lie about it, and refuses to talk about it without excessive outbursts of anger? And what if knowledge of the issue would cause a split in the church if it got out?

Sometimes, a split in the church is unavoidable. Divisions must come, Paul said (1 Cor. 11:19). He did not mean that God approved of divisions; only that carnality in the church leads inevitably to trouble. Paul called for vigilance, because the church's worst enemies arise from within the congregation (Acts 20:30). Warnings about them were a refrain in Paul's letters. "Watch out for those who cause divisions and put obstacles in your way that are contrary to the teaching you have learned. Keep away from them" (Rom. 16:17). "Warn a divisive person once, and then warn them a second time. After that, have nothing to do with them" (Titus 3:10).

In some cases, excommunication of a chronic troublemaker is the only way to restore the church to health. In other cases, as suggested in the texts listed here and in the principal passage on the subject (Matt. 18:15–20), the sin is not of such a nature as to require immediate excommunication but rather isolation of some kind. "Treat them as you would a pagan or a tax collector."

Sooner or later the church will know about the conflict to which you refer. You cannot keep it secret. So bite the bullet and enlist the help of a friend or two, and if they cannot get through to the troublemaker, go to the elders.

—D. C.

93. Why do young people refuse to believe that the rules laid down by their parents really are good rules? I don't mean simply rules about cleaning their rooms or washing their hands before eating, but the rules like not drinking or taking drugs and abstaining from premarital sex.

Like countless generations before them, young people today want to know for themselves whether or not something is good for them. Mom or Dad can lay down the law about what's good or bad, but kids think there's nothing as certain as experiencing it for themselves. Then they'll know for sure. But they are wrong. Unfortunately, some will suffer the consequences of doing what is absolutely wrong. Illicit booze and drugs and sex can lead to addiction, disease, a criminal record, and a wake of destruction. It's difficult to recover from these consequences apart from the miraculous grace of God.

As parents, grandparents, and other loving adults, what can we do to keep our precious children from falling prey to these temptations? First, we must recognize that these sins are not new today (see 1 Cor. 10:13). Second, we must encourage our children to be immersed in a lifestyle of faith, including prayer for God's guidance, habits of studying Scripture, and a community of godly friends (see Prov. 12:26). And finally, we should commit to praying for our children throughout their lives, asking God to protect them and to restore them if they have fallen from a path of righteousness (see Luke 15:11–32).

—M. K.

94. Is suicide one of God's ways to take a believer home to Heaven?

The question is improperly framed. Suicide is the killing of one's self. It is wrong; it is the destruction of life, which is God's gift to us. How could killing it be "God's way" to take us home to Heaven?

For many individuals, however, including some Christians, the circumstances of life are so wretched that they do not see life as a gift. They see it as a curse from which they wish to escape. The painful quality of life they experience is a powerful motive for easy suicide. Nevertheless, the killing of oneself remains a sin.

It cannot be "one of God's ways to take a believer home to Heaven." Yet death by any means—whether by automobile accident, cancer, or suicide—is the door through which God's people enter Heaven. Believers who commit suicide go to Heaven; God does not block their way. Heaven is not gained by a worthy death or forfeited by an unworthy death; entrance is secured by union with Christ through faith. So, the question should ask whether suicide is "one of God's *approved* ways to enter Heaven." And to that question, the answer is no.

—D. C.

95. I am a Christian teenager wondering what to do when one of my parents, who claims to be a Christian, is living a sinful lifestyle. My parent is loving and provides for me but has made many life choices that are biblically wrong while continuing to use Christian language and talk about Jesus in warm, personal ways. Is it my place to speak up?

This is a painful position to be in, one I have seen often in my teaching career: young adults who follow God obediently while being let down by their parental models. That you have remained true to God is a work of grace.

Certainly you should continue to pray faithfully. While you should honor your parent for what he or she does well, I think there is a place for respectfully expressing your sadness over his or her choices and the way those affect you. Ideally, it would be good if a Christian adult whom your parent respects could point out these inconsistencies between proclamation and practice.

We should remember that Jesus taught that honoring parents was no excuse for failing to honor God. Following Him requires putting Him above all others, including mothers and fathers. That may mean that you cannot join your parent in certain activities, opinions, or discussions. And if his or her lifestyle runs any danger of weakening your Christian resolve, it might be necessary to separate yourself physically from the situation. Finally, if possible, find older Christians to parent you spiritually, someone with whom you can talk through the dilemmas you encounter and the decisions you make.

—R. d.

96. My friend says that if you're living a life of victory in Christ, you will no longer be tempted, but that certainly has not been the case in my life. Why is that?

It is a wonderful thing to live a life that says no to sin, but any honest believer will tell you that temptation is a real "spiritual disease" that we will constantly fight. The necessity to say no will always be there. Scripture makes it clear that we regularly battle the world, the flesh, and the devil. As much as we'd like to believe that at some point in our Christian life we will be immune to thoughts of doing wrong, neither the Bible nor our own experiences back that up.

Young people struggling with the sins of alcoholism, drugs, or promiscuity who rededicate their lives to Christ are often under the impression that once they've made that decision they will no longer struggle with their besetting sins again. Those battling homosexual behavior, for example, are convinced that their decision to follow Christ will eradicate their sinful desires. When the impulse to sin comes around again, they feel it's obvious Christ is really not a part of their lives or can do nothing about their sinful behavior, and they fall back into their gay lifestyle. The problem for many is the mistaken notion that temptation itself is the sin. They've confused temptation with the sin itself.

James said that we should consider it joy when we are tempted or tested (see James 1:2). If temptation were the actual sin, how could we find that joyful? Here's what Scripture means: the testing or temptation is an opportunity to prove that the Spirit of God is in you to overwhelm evil desires.

James goes on to say, "Blessed is the one who perseveres under trial because, having stood the test, that person will receive the crown of life that the Lord has promised to those who love him" (1:12). The only way to overwhelm our sin is to submit ourselves to God. The idea of submission involves a tender heart willing to be obedient. Our submission is actualized in our obedience.

Yes, there will be times of failure, and the Word reminds us that we have an Advocate with the Father, Jesus Christ (see 1 John 2:1). And when we sin, He tells us to confess the sin, and He is faithful and just to forgive us our sin (see 1 John 1:9).

We are in a battle. When some suggest that at some point in time, this side of Heaven, the battle with temptation is over, they are wrong. Dead wrong. But it doesn't mean that Christ can't bring about His victory in and through us. He certainly can!

—D. C.

97. Does the Bible actually forbid having sex before marriage?

Yes. The Bible says that virginity before marriage is a true virtue. Compare that to the lifestyles of the "rich and famous" and even all the people like us, a little closer to home. Today sex has been trivialized for both young men and women, and what should have been presented to our chosen one as a special gift has been shared with so many others that it has lost its sacred meaning. Both men and women should keep themselves pure for their marriage. Purity is not just for women. The New Testament repeatedly stresses that sexual immorality is not consistent with a life that honors God (see 1 Cor. 6:18; Gal. 5:19; Eph. 5:3; 1 Thess. 4:3).

—*M. K.*

98. Our daughter joined a cult. Previously (until she went to college), she was a good Christian girl. She is a different person— unreasonable and unloving, though she says her new friends are more loving than any Christians she knows. Is she lost forever? My heart is broken.

Lost, yes. Forever lost? Not unless she chooses to be lost forever. Have you never read the story of the prodigal son (Luke 15:11–32)? That young fool left home but eventually came to his senses and returned to the father he had treated so vilely. His father was waiting for him, which is the point of the story. Repentant prodigals are a dime a dozen. A waiting father—in this case the heavenly Father—is a miracle of grace.

The apostle Paul is scornful of perverted teachers who "destroy the faith of some" (2 Tim. 2:18). Nevertheless, Paul immediately encourages us with these statements, "The Lord knows those who are his," and that some, responding to the help of sensible believers, "will come to their senses and escape from the trap of the devil" (vv. 19, 26). The Lord knows them, even if they do not know that they are His. In my judgment, this passage seems to indicate that it is possible for one to lose his or her faith for a time, yet not that vital connection with the Lord that, ultimately, is the Holy Spirit's to maintain.

Your prayer should be that your daughter meets believers who will help her come to her senses. You can pray in the assurance that God will do everything divinely possible (in keeping with His character) to rescue your daughter.

—D. C.

99. Malachi 3:10 says, " 'Bring the whole tithe into the storehouse, that there may be food in my house. Test me in this,' says the LORD Almighty, 'and see if I will not throw open the floodgates of heaven and pour out so much blessing that there will not be room enough to store it.' " Does this mean everybody is supposed to tithe?

This verse was written to an agricultural economy based on the work people did in their fields. But Christians today don't just grow crops to survive. So we, for the most part, have never brought to the church our cabbages and corn and grain as our tithe. (Maybe at a church fellowship supper!) These words were meant for Jews who brought their produce as offerings for the priests in Israel.

In the early days of the church there was no enforced tithe, but we see in Acts 2 that actually people were contributing all that they had, including profits from the sale of property, to the church. Since then, many Christians have found that offering God 10 percent of their income provides a helpful guideline to keep them accountable to give back to the Lord. But the primary New Testament principle of giving is found in 2 Corinthians 9. We are to give cheerfully and faithfully.

Some Christians are so cash-strapped by debt they think it is impossible to give to the Lord. When our overhead gets out of hand because of our confusion of wants and needs, we discover that giving to God helps bring discipline to our lives and puts our wants in true perspective.

—M. K.

100. My parents object to my dating a non-Christian. They say it is wrong. But he is a very good man, and if no Christian girl dates him, how will he hear the Word and be saved?

People generally marry the kind of people they date, and a Christian who marries a non-Christian disobeys God's Word about the "unequal yoke" described in 2 Corinthians 6:14–16. Many people hear the gospel from sources other than their dates. It would be much wiser to leave the witnessing to a member of his own gender.

—*D. C.*

101. How can we stop rock and roll music in church? I hate it.

Years ago, one of my sons told me I was clueless—that I thought that virtually anything noisy and banal and that got young girls screaming was rock and roll. Not so, he said: rock and roll is a genre in its own right, and it is not "played" in churches. Maybe you just hate ear-splitting racket and lump every kind under the label "rock and roll" or "Christian rock."

I, too, hate ear-splitting racket, especially in church, where it is inappropriate. I like ragtime and country music, but these also would be inappropriate in the kind of churches I frequent. It is a question of decorum and acceptable definitions of worship. But tastes differ, and many churches cater to young people who *like* rackety music and *respond* to it. Your tastes (maybe mine too) repel them; they think the sound is funereal. It gives them the willies. Terms such as appropriate, inappropriate, decorum, even worship, are defined differently in different places.

I grieve the loss of the old hymns—reverent and filled with theology and conducive to worship. But some of them are as banal as much of the modern, noisy stuff. Our children dismiss them as sentimental drivel, not a tenth as good as many new Christian songs.

Back to your question: how to stop rock and roll, or what

passes for it, in the church. It can't be done except by forming a church of geezers and grannies and nobody else.

—*D. C.*

102. If a Christian is living a life of faith and obeying the Word of God, is it really possible for him or her to ever be continually depressed? I have friends who have gone through serious crises that have knocked them for a loop. And it just doesn't seem right that Christians with mental illness or depression should ever have to take medication if they truly practiced their faith and believed.

What if I asked you if it were possible for a Christian to suffer from diabetes or heart disease or arthritis? Should this Christian go to a doctor for treatment, including a regular regimen of medication? Of course Christians can get sick, and it is perfectly appropriate for us to seek out the knowledge and skill of medical doctors for treatment. We still recognize that God is the Great Physician, but we are also thankful that He has given doctors the resources to treat the illnesses that afflict our bodies and minds.

Mental illness is very real, and medical science has provided medications and practices that help millions of people. Some people consider antidepressant drugs as a cop-out of faith. But for some patients, antidepressant drugs treat chemical imbalances in their bodies. Others may be helped by paying attention to God's principles for a healthy life and godly life, following guidelines of rest and dealing with stress. But the bottom line is that it's all about God.

A time is coming when there will be no more sickness or death, but this side of Heaven we often find ourselves in the midst of a valley of tears with much physical pain and emotional suffering. You may be thinking, "Can't we just pray and ask God to provide an instant cure to remove a particular thorn in our flesh or soul that we're dealing with?" And of course we can ask God for a miracle. We can also accept the miracle He has already provided in medications He has allowed men and women to research and develop that have helped countless patients overcome disease or live with both physical and mental illness. We can thank God for all that!

—*M. K.*

103. What do you think about Christian's watching R-rated movies?

I think that Christians should stay away from most of the R-rated films. Watching these films can destroy our personal sensitivity to sin. Years ago we used to tell believers they are better off if they stay out of theaters altogether. But today that's almost a moot point, since television, DVDs, and the internet have brought many of those films directly into the home—and directly to children who watch them. Today, Christian websites even offer reviews of films that Christians might find appropriate for both their families and their values. In some ways this is quite a change of direction, from no movies at all to movies that pass muster.

But the truth is, the Christian life has always been about

choices. Is there anything wrong with staying away from movies completely? Absolutely not, especially if watching movies is something that you have always considered questionable, if not sinful. If your conscience is bothered by watching movies, then you should not feel compelled to go along with the crowd. If the subject matter of television and movies goes beyond what you're comfortable with, shut them down. If television or movies are a stumbling block for you, walk away from them. Your convictions are commendable.

—*M. K.*

104. Why is it that many pro-life advocates support the death penalty? They are opposed to killing an unborn baby, but they have no problem killing criminals. And then some pro-choice advocates have no problem destroying a fetus, but they can't stand the thought of giving a murderer his just deserts. In those cases, they look more "pro-life."

Well, first let me say that the Bible is pro-life. It certainly does not condone the aborting of an unborn baby. God sees life as precious. Yet God has given to government the ability to enforce capital punishment. Old Testament law went so far as to give the nation the right to execute not only murderers but also adulterers, those who abuse their parents, rebellious children, people who intentionally violated the Sabbath, and other various and sundry things as well.

The New Testament, however, doesn't explicitly discuss the

death penalty, but it does state that God has established governments and given them the authority to make decisions that individuals do not have. The right to inflict death on murderers was never given to individuals but only to governments who ultimately will be held accountable to God. As individuals we are not to kill or inflict vengeance—including the lives of the unborn or those who have committed crimes or harmed others in some way.

—*M. K.*

105. Is it wrong or is it okay to donate your organs at death?

How can it be wrong? A dying person has no more use for them, and by donating them may give the recipient many years of useful life. The apostle John says that Jesus "laid down his life for us. And we ought to lay down our lives for our brothers and sisters" (1 John 3:16). He means that if circumstances call for it, we should be willing to die as Jesus died—literally, not figuratively—for our brothers and sisters. If giving our lives for someone in the family of God may be required of us, how can we then quibble about giving organs for which we will have no further use?

Some people shrink from dismemberment after death; they wish to be buried whole, lest they be resurrected permanently impaired. But that is a pagan sentiment, unworthy of Christians. We know that God's work of resurrecting our bodies does not depend on their intact burial.

—*D. C.*

106. Is it okay for a Christian to use profane language? Some Christians have a problem with people using it, but other Christians think profanity isn't an issue.

Our Lord is concerned about our use of language. The Bible says, "Do not let any unwholesome talk come out of your mouths, but only what is helpful for building others up according to their needs, that it may benefit those who listen" (Eph. 4:29). Does profanity fit the category of unwholesome talk? Yes. Profanity shows contempt or disrespect, a lack of reverence for God or respect for others. It is sin to use words to disrespect God (Ex. 20:7) and to show contempt for people (Matt. 5:21–23; James 3:1–12). Sin has impacted and twisted every aspect of our personhood, even the way we use language (Ps. 12:1–4; Rom. 3:13–14).

There is hope. Faith in Christ and new birth result in substantial healing in a person, and one of those areas is the way we use words, language, and the transformation of the content of our conversation. We change the way we use words as an expression of cleansing of our hearts; the way we use language indicates what is in our hearts.

The conversation of a Christian and the conversation of an unsaved person should be qualitatively different. Scripture says, "Let your conversation be always full of grace, seasoned with salt, so that you may know how to answer everyone" (Col. 4:6). Note that graceful speech should always characterize the words of the follower of Christ. The image of salt helps us understand that language itself can be corrupt, rotten, and give off a bad moral odor. Salt is a preservative. Our conversation should retard corruption, slow down decay, and act as a preserving power in our world. This is a tall order for language.

Some struggle with the seriousness of how we use language because we live in a culture that does not value words. Often we hear expressions like "Oh, that's just rhetoric," or "Those are just words." But words matter, and our use of words matters deeply to God. Words reveal character (Matt. 12:33–34); we will give account to God for the way we have used words in this life; every word that a Christian utters should be spoken in the name of Christ (Col. 3:17).

In short, profanity abuses the gift of language and indicates a heart that is not in fellowship with God. In a fallen world where vicious and mean words are spoken every day, is our use of words distinctive? Is there something heavenly, wholesome, and winsome about our verbal interactions with people that point them to Christ? Given our responsibility before the Lord to use words that express our new heart and new life in Christ, serious reflection on the following verse may be helpful: "May these words of my mouth and this meditation of my heart be pleasing in your sight, LORD, my Rock and my Redeemer" (Ps. 19:14).

—*W. N.*

107. Is the "faith promise" plan of raising support for its mission's program scriptural? A few of the members of our church say that it is unscriptural.

How do you define "scriptural"? As the term is commonly used, an activity is scriptural only if it was practiced in the first-century churches described in the Bible. But things not done in Bible times are not necessarily *unscriptural.* They might be *extrascriptural* and yet fully acceptable. Reasonable people do not object to Sunday schools or mission conferences and many other things not done in ancient times yet eminently useful in modern times.

The "faith promise" plan can be considered unscriptural only if it violates a clearly discerned Bible principle. I can think of only two possibly legitimate complaints: first, the temptation to urge believers to give more than they actually have, or reasonably expect to have; and, second, the basing of the mission budget on the expectation of receiving a promised yet sometimes unrealistic amount. Pledges and faith promises, which are essentially the same thing, may or may not be kept.

Mission planners need to remember two principles: first, a budget based on faith promises is not proof of faith; it is presumption. God is not committed to supplying the money we think we need. Second, pressure on the Lord's people to give more than they think they can give dishonors them. As Paul says, "For if the willingness is there, the gift is acceptable *according to what one has, not according to what one does not have*" (2 Cor. 8:12, italics added).

—D. C.

108. The Bible says, "godliness has value for all things" (1 Tim. 4:8). What is godliness?

Godliness is devotion to the person of God. It is a comprehensive term for the whole of the Christian life. Godliness includes knowledge of God and not merely knowledge about

God. Godliness also includes reverence for God and loyalty to God. It is the response of heart in all of life to who God is in His awesome holiness and unspeakable glory.

—*W. N.*

109. Why do Christians who have gone to church for years and been involved in ministry just stop going?

There is no one answer to this question. I have seen people who were integral parts of a church stop going for any number of reasons, including disillusionment (perhaps a church split or treatment by a pastor), because of burnout from over involvement, because of a life circumstance (divorce is an oft-cited example), or because of a crisis in their faith, to name a few. In her book, *Quitting Church*, author Julia Duin asks a similar question and among other things calls for better teaching, preaching, and pastors in touch with the lives of their worshipers—in short, for better churches, where "community" is cultivated. I think this is an apt analysis, especially her emphasis on good teaching and a congregation and pastor who mutually care for each other.

Christians with a history of committed church attendance really don't "just stop going" to church. Instead, over time, they sustain small, uncared-for spiritual bruises and fissures that become major injuries of the spirit. Doubtless, signs have been visible—an absence here or there, a gradual lessening of connection to others, a withdrawal from a key church activity. Sadly, such hints often go unnoticed or unremarked by the pastoral staff and fellow members. The disappointed, the hurt, and even the rebellious long to be seen and known, to feel that they are loved and that they matter. It is imperative for every one of us to live attentive lives, both in our own relationship to church and the things that might cause our estrangement from it and to what is going on in other peoples' lives. As Hebrews 10:24–25 says, "And let us consider how we may spur one another on toward love and good deeds, not giving up meeting together, as some are in the habit of doing, but encouraging one another—and all the more as you see the Day approaching."

—*R. d.*

110. What does the word carnal mean in 1 Corinthians 3? How can someone being described as "carnal" still be called a Christian?

Several years ago, a friend was jogging down one of the rural roads near our home. Looking on ahead, he saw a huge mound of butterflies near the upcoming intersection. He couldn't understand what it was until he actually came closer, and discovered this huge clump of butterflies feeding on road kill. He couldn't believe it. These glorious butterflies were eating from the decaying carcass of some unfortunate animal. As he resumed his run, he thought, "How like those butterflies Christians are—transformed by God, often feeding on the decaying detritus of this old world." He admitted that he too, was like them: often caught up in the filth of this world.

John MacArthur has said that he defines carnal Christians as people who are carnal in some things and yet make Spirit-filled decisions in other areas. He personally doesn't believe that a carnal Christian is a permanent state, and I would agree. There are times when spiritual people, genuinely born-again men and women, are controlled by the things of this world. The truth is that we all from time to time live carnal lives through our choices, which are not based on the Spirit of God within us but by the old nature. Paul wrote, "Brothers and sisters, I could not address you as people who live by the Spirit but as people who are still worldly—mere infants in Christ. . . . You are still worldly. For since there is jealousy and quarreling among you, are you not worldly?" (1 Cor. 3:1, 3).

I believe it is clear that Paul is actually addressing brothers and sisters in Christ. If a person is in a constant state of carnal living, he or she should probably examine their life, and ask, "Am I really a child of God at all?" When Paul was talking to people he considered "carnal Christians," he was speaking of those who at the time were being ruled by their flesh nature and not by the Spirit of God that dwells in authentic Christians. The child of God should readily know that he has messed up and should quickly confess his sin, restoring his fellowship with a holy God.

—*M. K.*

111. It seems that daily I hear or read something about homosexuality. I do not believe the practice has God's approval, but could you point me to some biblical texts that deal with this issue?

The question of homosexuality confronts us almost daily on the internet, in textbooks, courtrooms, films, legislatures, magazines, newspapers, schools, and the streets. It is one of the burning issues of the early twenty-first-century world. It is imperative that we go to the Bible, God's Word, in order to ascertain what God thinks about homosexuality.

A number of passages in the Old and the New Testament deal directly with this question: Leviticus 20:13; Romans 1:26–27; 1 Corinthians 6:9–11; and 1 Timothy 1:9–10. In Leviticus 18:22 (NLT) the Lord Himself says, "Do not practice homosexuality . . . it is a detestable sin." In the Old Testament law the penalty for a homosexual act was death (Lev. 20:13). In Romans 1:26–27, homosexual desires and practices are condemned and are evidence of the universal rejection of God's will and revelation. In 1 Corinthians 6:9–11, Scripture asserts that the practice of homosexuality is not consistent with sanctification. The witness of Scripture is clear that God declares these practices to be a sinful perversion of His good gifts to His creation.

—W. N.

112. Can a homosexual be delivered from this lifestyle?

Thank God, yes! Jesus died on the cross for the sins of all people (1 Cor. 15:3; Gal. 1:4; 1 Tim. 2:5–6, 1 John 2:2). It is the wonder and miracle of God's heart that He loves sinners and gave His Son to die on the cross for the sins of the entire human family. As His children, we are responsible to love all people (1 Thess. 3:12).

We know that we, too, are redeemed from sin, and we must lovingly offer the gospel of grace and call those who live in sin to repentance and faith in Christ. In the Corinthian church, some believers there had lived in homosexual sin prior to their conversion. But Paul says to them: "And that is what some of you *were*. But you were washed, you were sanctified, you were justified in the name of the Lord Jesus Christ and by the Spirit of our God" (1 Cor. 6:11). I am so deeply thankful that Christ can deliver us from the guilt, penalty, and power of any sin!

—*W. N.*

113. Does the Bible say when the age of accountability begins? In Judaism, a boy becomes a man at age thirteen, so is this the age of accountability?

Presumably you're asking when a child becomes responsible for his or her sins and, therefore, must be converted (i.e., born again) or risk damnation in the event of death. Only God knows the answer to that question, and the Bible does not answer it. Scripture speaks of accountability with reference to adults. Check passages such as Matthew 12:36; 25:14–30; and all the sermons or proclamations of the gospel in Acts.

The plain truth is that we do not know the age at which any particular child is mature enough to know that he or she must repent and believe the gospel for forgiveness. It seems to me that we cannot set an age that applies to every person as the age of accountability. In any case, should a child die prior to having this understanding, we can trust in the grace and mercy of God that little children do not go to Hell.

—*D. C.*

114. Since Jesus taught that we are to be merciful (Matt. 5:7), would it not be obedience to Him to assist an aged, suffering, or terminally ill person in dying?

Although mercy is certainly a commendable virtue, with regard to euthanasia (literally, "good death"), it allows a fallible person to usurp the prerogative and responsibility of God alone. Believers must remember the following biblical principles when considering "mercy killing."

First, all people are made in the image of God (Gen. 1:26), and therefore God demands that all human life be treated as sacred. Taking a life without cause rejects the sacred nature of life. Therefore, the image of God in humanity is the basis for forbidding murder (Gen. 9:6).

Second, according to the Scriptures, God alone is sovereign over life and death. For example, Deuteronomy 32:39 says: "See now that I myself am he! There is no god besides me. I put to death and I bring to life, I have wounded and I will heal." God alone creates life, and He alone has the authority to take it. The psalmist also marvels at a God who is so sovereign that He determines not only the beginning of our lives but the end of them as well: "All the days ordained for me were written in your book before one of them came to be" (Ps. 139:16). Human beings are not to shorten God's determined lifespan in other people.

Third, God uses suffering to accomplish His purposes in our lives. "We also glory in our sufferings, because we know that suffering produces perseverance; perseverance, character; and character, hope" (Rom. 5:3–4). Even in all his suffering, Job did not attempt to cut short his life; instead, he used the occasion of his physical and emotional torment to beseech God. We are not to short-circuit God's purposes in our lives.

In light of the above perspective, how should we care for the suffering and the terminally ill? One step to take is to provide painkilling medications to limit their pain and suffering (see Prov. 31:6). We should also distinguish between "mercy killing" and "mercy dying." Mercy killing wrongly puts people to death to alleviate suffering. Mercy dying allows people to die by not taking extraordinary measures to preserve life. It allows God to take someone mercifully rather than artificially prolonging life. In the end, it is the One in whom "we live and move and have our being" (Acts 17:28) who determines both the beginning and the end of our lives.

—*M. R.*

115. Is it okay for Christians to take political action? Or must we be 100 percent passive?

Our system of government cannot function properly without the participation of intelligent people. Purely passive citizens who turn a blind eye encourage corruption. Thus, we Christians ought to make our voices heard. But we ought to do it in civilized (i.e., Christian) fashion. The standards of conduct governing the ministry of the Word of God should guide and control our political conduct (2 Cor. 2:17; 4:1–2). Passivity or plain old inertia is unbecoming in Christians in any sphere, including politics.

—*D. C.*

116. Over many years I've experienced depression that comes and goes. I know that in the years when I didn't have hope, Hope had me. I have seen God working in my life, but lately depression is getting hold of me again. I'm scared and don't know how to get my mind focused on the right things.

One of the most comforting things for me when I find the circumstances of my life overwhelming is to begin to read the Psalms. While much of the Bible speaks *to* us, the Psalms seem to speak *for* us. I can't tell you how many times in reading the book of Psalms I was astonished to discover that the writers were putting into words the feelings that I had felt. It dawned on me that my experiences were very similar to these spokesmen for God. They'd been where I'd been, felt what I felt. It was a comfort to know that others have experienced some of what I have and made it through because of the presence of a mighty and caring God.

I love reading the Psalms and also memorizing Scripture. Both enable me to replace the negative thoughts that want to consume me with the positive expressions of Scripture. My prayer is that you will allow Christ to overwhelm the experiences of this old life. "Demolish arguments and every pretention that sets itself up against the knowledge of God, and . . . take captive every thought to make it obedient to Christ" (2 Cor. 10:5).

—*M. K.*

117. I struggle with passages of Scripture that instruct us to honor our parents. My father lived a destructive lifestyle when I was growing up, and as an adult, the memories of his behavior during my childhood come back and I become angry. I don't think my father merits honor. What am I to do?

Your father apparently made some bad choices when you were growing up, and painful memories are still with you. My heart goes out to you. Your question is valid. Among the Ten Commandments (Ex. 20:1–17; Deut. 5:6–21), the command to honor our father and our mother is the fifth commandment, and it is the first commandment to deal with human relationships (Ex. 20:12; Deut. 5:16). The first four commandments deal with our relationship with God, and the last six deal with our relationship with people. Our relationship with the Lord should express itself in our relationships with people, beginning with our attitude toward our parents.

The fifth commandment is repeated in the New Testament: "'Honor your father and mother'—which is the first commandment with a promise—'so that it may go well with you and that you may enjoy long life on the earth'" (Eph. 6:2–3). While obedience to God's Word always leads to blessing in some way, the fifth commandment is the first of the Ten Commandments with an explicit promise from God. God promises that we will have a better life when we put this command into practice. Honoring our parents impacts the quality and length of our lives. Next to our relationship with God, our relationship with our parents is the foundation for the development of other healthy human relationships. To honor our parents means to respect them, to cherish them, and to value them.

How can we honor a parent or parents who in our estimation do not merit such respect or honor? Well, the concern here is not the merit of the parents. The concern here is obedience to the Lord. We honor our parents because God tells us to do so. It is not a matter of the merit of the parents but an issue of obedience to God. In the context of Ephesians 6, the honoring of our parents is the result of being filled with the Holy Spirit. God is not calling us to honor our parents in our own strength. As we walk with God in the power of the Holy Spirit, the Spirit Himself enables us to obey God and His Word. I am not saying that obedience to the Lord in this matter will be easy for you or that you will ever have the best relationship with your dad, but by God's grace you can respect him and honor him. Your attitude toward him can become an attitude that glorifies God, and by the grace of God you will consequently become a better person. I know you still hurt sometimes, but I want to say in all compassion that God's grace is sufficient for you (2 Cor. 12:9).

—*W. N.*

118. Why doesn't our church grow? God's Word is proclaimed, and I believe all the members are decent, God-fearing people, faithful in the Christian life. We are willing to try new methods.

Righteous living by a church's members does not ensure numerical growth. Our Lord addressed His disciples as a "little flock" (Luke 12:32). Of course, that was before Pentecost, when thousands poured into the new church in Jerusalem. Even so, most if not all churches in New Testament times seem to have been small groups of people. Both large and small churches often include people whose lives are disgraceful. Why most churches remain numerically stagnant whereas a few explode numerically is a question ventilated in many books and other resources about church growth. Most importantly, though, remember that there are different kinds of growth, including coveted growth in the knowledge of God and resultant spiritual maturity.

You need not feel guilty if your church is small—unless of course, you are small because you are not friendly or are lazy or locked into sectarian traditions that have little to offer ordinary believers in search of a church home for themselves and their children.

—*D. C.*

119. As a middle-aged woman in the church, I often have young women and men ask me about the disappointments of life, particularly the problem of not having found a mate. A young woman has said to me, "I won't be able to bear it if I don't find someone, especially since I have prayed so hard." Or, I hear, "My friends all have someone, and they aren't even Christians." How do I answer the hard questions?

I understand this dilemma since, as a professor, I work with young people, ones who not only have this understandable question but who also wonder why God has allowed them to suffer heartbreak in their childhood. The thing one must not do in these situations is to tell him or her (or anyone for that matter) that you're sure he or she will find someone someday, to just keep obeying God because He will reward that obedience, or cite that too easily quoted, often-used-out-of-context verse, "in all things God works for the good of those who love him," as a quick answer to deep, undeserved distress. The truth of the matter is that suffering exists; bad things happen to children and "good people"; and a person may or may not get married, may or may not have a good marriage, may or may not experience circumstantial happiness and success in life.

The foundational issue each one of us has to come to terms with and remind ourselves of regularly is our theology of God—what we believe about Him. If we believe firmly that He is good, we can accept disappointment much better (though not without pain) than those who have never dealt biblically and personally with who He is.

The entire book of Job is about Job coming to terms in a whole new way with a God he has believed in and served faithfully. He has to do this because of the intense suffering and loss he goes through. God gives him no lists of reasons for his extreme reversals of fortune and rebukes the friends that do. After listening to Job speak his suffering and his anguished questions and self-defense, God points back to Himself by asking Job a series of rhetorical questions that fill four chapters (38–41). All of God's questions draw such an overpowering picture of the omnipotent, omnipresent, and omniscient God that Job, brought back (or, more accurately, pushed forward) to a new level of spiritual comprehension, answers, "I know that you can do all things; no purpose of yours can be thwarted" (42:2); "My ears had heard of you but now my eyes have seen you" (42:5).

German theologian Helmut Thielicke tells the story of a man who lost his four children, one after another, in two weeks. The man wrote poignantly about the way he committed each one of them to the "fatherly hands of God." In what Thielicke calls this "ghastly trial of faith," this man [like Job] never broke his conversation with God and so never yielded to "that dumb, leaden silence" by which so many of us are tempted in the darkest hours of our lives. He turned his worst tragedy into prayer, a prayer to a God he believed was good. This belief was born out of knowing His Word and character and developing a trusting relationship. Then he could take all joys and sorrows to God. Such ability to turn tragedy to prayer came from a decision made more and more decisively through the years.

I am reminded of the words to the old hymn by Daniel W. Whittle: "But I know whom I have believed / And am persuaded that He is able / To keep that which I've committed / Unto Him against that day."

—R. d.

120. At church our preacher often talks about being "good stewards of money." I understand about tithing, but very little specific teaching is given about how to think about money besides that.

Actually, Scripture does give us a specific, foundational approach to money. Matthew 6:21 says, "Where your treasure is, there your heart will be also," a principle that applies whether or not you're a Christian. Heart follows treasure. Christ talked about money, and the book of Proverbs is full of references to using money foolishly and wisely.

Martin Luther observed, "There are three conversions necessary: the conversion of the heart, mind, and the purse." As Christians we must acknowledge that God owns 100 percent of our money, not just our tithe, a principle so obvious it seems like a cliché. That is the most crucial way to think about money. This enriches our relationship with Him, deepens our understanding of how to use what we have, and delivers us from frivolous waste on one side and rigid frugality on the other. Scripture never tells us not to enjoy what God has given us. It just tells us to use it prudently and thoughtfully in keeping with our Christian values.

Oddly enough, this principle is not as commonly considered as one would think. We live divided lives, doing our Christian duty through tithing (and many Christians do not even do that) and then, perhaps affected by the culture, operate randomly in regard to what's left. Yet, how we spend our money says a great deal about our vision of life and how rooted it is in our faith.

—*R. d.*

121. How can I get my husband to tithe? I want us as a married couple and new parents to live with God at the center

and do what He wants us to do, and I want my husband to be with me on this. What do I do?

You have already done well. There is probably not a lot more that you can do about this except pray. I'm assuming your husband is a Christian. If he is not, he has a lot more on his plate to deal with than simply not tithing. He needs Jesus as His Savior.

You wouldn't be the first person to have a husband who found it difficult to tithe. Tithing is about obedience, but your husband has to learn that for himself. Women tend to be much more sensitive to things like this than most men. Many men are pragmatic and want immediate results from their expenditures. Tithing seems illogical.

If you have a job outside the home, you might begin to tithe from the money that you bring into the home yourself. If your husband attends a good Bible-believing church, pray that he absorbs what is being taught about stewardship. Information from a stewardship ministry might be helpful, but try not to nag when it comes to discussing stewardship. He knows where you stand.

Maybe you could suggest that you give 5 percent of the family income to the Lord's work as a starter, instead of 10 percent. It might be a way of teaching your husband how to let go of what he considers his money. Whatever you do, don't give your husband the idea that tithing will mean big bucks down the road. If we give, God may give us more money, but it's so that we are in a position to give even more to Him, not necessarily to bank or spend (2 Cor. 9:8–9).

—D. C.

122. I recently was baptized in another church after growing up in a Catholic church. I seem to have brought on rejection and even hostility from my friends and family because they feel I'm deserting my faith. How can I respond?

Being baptized, I believe, is an act of obedience for all believers. It is for those who truly understand what it means to be born again and are indwelt with the Holy Spirit, as all believers are. It is hard on those who love you when they feel you are rejecting the faith of your family. You are not rejecting your belief in Jesus Christ. Your baptism as an adult, though, is an affirmation of genuine faith that may or may not have been there as a child.

Be kind to those who are hard on you and reject you. Taking a stand on a biblical issue is important, but the mark of a true believer is how we respond. It should be in love. Godly love is the only thing that will enable you to communicate God's truth to them. I hope you are surrounded by brothers and sisters in a local church who will encourage you and uphold you in prayer.

—*D. C.*

123. Is it okay for Christians to go on strike?

Yes, with some reservations. Bible students who say, "No, it is not okay," point to Ephesians 6:5–8 and Colossians 3:22–25 as the definitive answer to the question. In those texts, slaves are told to obey their masters—which is interpreted as, "No, do not strike." But a slave's relationship with his master (i.e., owner) is not analogous to an ordinary employee's relationship with the shop or company for which he works.

The question implies employment in a union shop, in which case the question should have been asked before taking the job. For employment in a union shop, the job seeker concedes a measure of control over his or her job to the local union. This includes automatic deduction of dues *and* the decision to strike. If, after a vote, the union bosses call for a strike, the members are obliged to go on strike. Only if a Christian decides that the strike is *morally wrong* should he refuse to join the strike, in which case he should be prepared to pay whatever penalty may be imposed for breaking ranks.

For information about the rights and obligations of a union member, and the penalty for breaking ranks, one should consult a labor lawyer. But if possible, do it before taking the job.

—*D. C.*

124. I have been a Christian for years and am in a drought spiritually. I want to study God's Word but do not know how. What do you suggest?

First, a word of encouragement: occasional times of spiritual "drought" (i.e., loss of appetite for or enjoyment of spiritual things) are not uncommon. They are part of the rhythm of life. The tide comes in and then goes out. The moon waxes and then wanes. Rhythm in nature is matched by rhythm in our emotional and spiritual lives. We all experience bouts of physical and spiritual weariness. We don't want to read or pray. Spiritual "drought" is the counterpart to physical weariness, but we need not be mired in that unhappy condition. Maturity is the ability to control the rhythm lest we stay listless.

The question assumes correctly that Bible study is a vital part in the work of recovering the joy of the Lord (Neh. 8:10; Ps. 51:8, 12–13).

It is one of several spiritual disciplines critical to a consistently fresh (as opposed to stale) Christian experience. If the Bible has begun to bore you, here is the first thing you might find helpful: find a different version of Scripture than the one you habitually read. If your version is the NASB, switch to the NIV or vice versa. Try the NKJV or the ESV. By all means, read the NLT. If this way of identifying translations is new to you, ask a salesclerk in a Christian bookstore for help or check online. (All these versions and more are available at Biblegateway.com and the app YouVersion.) Renderings new to you will focus attention on the text, and you may see things hitherto overlooked. The Bible will come alive.

Here is the second step toward renewal of vital Bible study: reduce the time you spend watching television. Note: I say, "reduce," because I would not think that many believers will cut out television completely. But everybody who hates spiritual dryness and wants to read the Bible knows without being told that he or she *must* control the television. There is no better way to make time for studying the Bible than to take it from television time.

—D. C.

125. One of my friends is discouraged because he struggles with temptation. How can I help him?

All Christians, even godly Christians, have experienced or are experiencing or will experience temptation of some kind. None of us are exempt from temptation this side of Heaven. We must remind ourselves that temptation is not sin. Sin is yielding to or giving in to temptation. The issue, then, is not how to live a life free of temptation, but how to be victorious over temptation in our experience.

Here are three truths that will help your friend. First, our temptations are not unique (1 Cor. 10:13a). Others have experienced or are experiencing similar struggles. Second, by the grace of God we can handle every temptation that comes into our life (1 Cor. 10:13b, c). Third, God will always make a way for us to escape temptation's snare (1 Cor. 10:13d, e). Encourage your friend to implement the following strategy: resist temptation immediately, pray for strength, delight in God, and take God's way of escape. Victory is ours in Jesus!

—*W. N.*

126. So much seems wrong in our culture today. I feel like it's a struggle to get things done well, to get polite treatment in public institutions, and to hold people to the promises they have made. But I hesitate at times to speak up because it seems like we're told as Christians to be nice. I need to know how to think about this.

I so appreciate this question. Christians often reflect the worst patterns of our culture. Somehow being nice, defined as being pleasant or not ruffling feathers, is mistakenly interpreted as how the gifts of the Spirit should be exercised. That kind of niceness may just be indifference or a desire to avoid conflict.

I once heard someone say, "Silence may be golden, but it can also be yellow." I can't help thinking of an intelligent essay titled "Why Don't We Complain?" by William F. Buckley Jr. He bemoans the silence of the average consumer and citizen. Complaining, he implies, is not necessarily negative or petty. It can mean making your voice heard so that you and other people will benefit from things done well and in order.

Think about the word *courage*, one of the four chief cardinal virtues, also called fortitude, which is the capacity to do what is right or necessary even in the face of adversity or discomfort. We cannot live cowed by the laziness or shrillness of culture. Christ never did. We must confront evil and sloppiness when we see it; we must speak up because our small protest may make a difference. We cannot adopt a neutral posture that tolerates small and large abuses in and out of the church. Speaking up just may be an issue of moral life or death.

—*R. d.*

127. My husband cheats a little on our federal taxes and asks me to sign the 1040 tax form. Every year, I am troubled by it. But recently I heard a sermon in which the preacher extolled Sarah for obeying Abraham. His point was that in obeying our husbands we wives obey God. The text was 1 Peter 3:3–6. Should I go on obeying my husband and sign the 1040 form?

No. As Peter himself said, under different circumstances, "Which is right in God's eyes: to listen to you, or to him? You be the judges!" (Acts 4:19). Paul tells us that each of us must answer to God for what we do (Rom. 14:12).

The text in 1 Peter 3 implies a rebuke of Sarah. Christian women are her daughters if "[they] do what is right and do not give way to fear," as Sarah did in Egypt. When Sarah obeyed Abraham and went docilely into the Pharaoh's harem, she did what was wrong, motivated by fear.

Why was Sapphira put to death? Does anyone doubt that in lying she was following orders from Ananias (Acts 5:1–11)? Docile, unquestioning obedience to a husband is not the will of God for women.

—*D. C.*

128. I received Christ as my personal Lord and Savior, and He has transformed my life. In light of these great realities in my experience, is being a part of a local church that important?

Yes, being a part of a local church is important. Of course, we are grateful to God for saving you and transforming your life. However, God has not called us to live the Christian life in isolation; He has called us to fellowship with other believers in the local church (Heb. 10:23–25).

In America we place such a great emphasis on our individuality that we may not appreciate the value that God places on local churches. Local churches were the first recipients of most of the letters of the New Testament. When we read these letters our tendency is to apply their imperatives and exhortations to our individual experience, when in fact the writers themselves gave these imperatives and exhortations to the community as a whole.

God intends for us to grow in the context of a local body of believers. He intends for us in some measure to reflect the mutual interpersonal relations of the Trinity in the context of local church life (John 17:20–23). Local churches are the primary context where we are to put the "one another" passages into practice (Gal. 5:13; Eph. 5:21; Phil. 2:3; 1 John 4:7–12). Living life in community with other followers of Christ is a part of our commitment to the Lord. I encourage you to become a part of a Christ-centered, Bible-believing and practicing local church. This is God's will for you in Christ Jesus.

—W. N.

PART THREE

Why isn't God mentioned in the book of Esther?

and other questions about
the Bible, who's in it,
and what it says

129. Do our beloved pets go to Heaven when they pass on? The Lord has given us thirteen acres of land where we have taken in rescue cats and dogs. He has given us these pets as companions. They are loyal and loving. Is there a place for them with Jesus?

I resonate deeply with the question, "Is there a place for them with Jesus?" In fact, when I was about nine, this was exactly my question, and I wrote to a well-known Bible program to find out the answer. Animals have a special place in our hearts; they *are* loyal and loving. I am so glad that today the greeting card market includes beautiful cards to send friends who lose pets.

To answer you, we know that in Genesis 1 God created animals and saw that they were "good" and "blessed them" and caused them to be "fruitful." He did this clearly for the beauty of the earth, for His delight and for that of men and women. In Genesis 2:19 He also asked Adam to name them, making them particular and important. As C. S. Lewis noted in *The Problem of Pain*, the Bible is silent on the matter of animals' immortality. While many of us have seen the intelligence of animals when they estimate just how far to jump or when to come running when they hear a food can open, we also know that their moral capacity is fundamentally different from human beings.

Still, animals are a central part of God's creation, and God has allowed them to bring us great joy. Though we don't know for sure whether our resurrected pets will be in Heaven, it seems likely animals will be part of the new heavens and new earth. In the words of Isaiah 11:6, "The wolf will live with the lamb, the leopard will lie down with the goat, the calf and the lion and the yearling together; and a little child will lead them." Perhaps Billy Graham was right when he answered the little girl who asked if her dog would be in Heaven: "If it would make you any happier, then he will be."

—R. d.

130. Reading through the New Testament, I came to the story of the demon-possessed man of the Gerasenes told in the gospels of Mark and Luke. I thought it was a really powerful story, but I wondered about a couple of things. Why did the demons ask to be sent into the pigs, and why did Jesus allow the demons to go into the pigs? Could He not just have destroyed them?

The details you note have often been seen as a controversial part of the narrative. In response to your first question, several possibilities exist. The demons, who can do nothing without God's permission, know they have been bested (see Mark 5:13). Perhaps they asked to be put into the pigs so they would have a bodily home for their evil activity and avoid being sent into the Abyss (place of torment). Or, perhaps, they wanted to continue their destruction, in the case of the pigs, knowing that would make trouble for Jesus. Demons are always bent on creating chaos.

The greater question is, as you note, why Jesus assented to this plan. After all, it does involve destruction of property and the livelihood of the pigs' owners. Here is where we see the love of God for individuals. We have to remember that the point of the story is not to destroy the demons but to deliver the demonized man from their power (Mark 5:19–20; Luke 8:39). As one commentator has noted, by sending the demons into the pigs, Jesus was giving proof that the demons had left the man, which was a profound gesture of mercy. When the people in the area saw those pig corpses floating in the lake and the man clothed and sane, no one could deny what had happened. More significantly, the man who was delivered, in the most dramatic deliverance given us in Scripture, would know that those demons were gone for good and feel supreme relief.

—R. d.

131. In a Bible Study last week, one of my friends said that Rahab, the woman who helped the Israelites bring down the walls of Jericho was not just an innkeeper but was also a prostitute. Can that be true?

Yes, women who were innkeepers then were often prostitutes. This woman had heard already (possibly from her traveling clients) how the Lord had worked in the lives of Israel, freeing them from Egypt by parting the Red Sea and enabling them to utterly defeat the Amorite rulers Sihon and Og. The people of Jericho were terrified of how God had empowered Judah.

She hid the two Israelite spies with the understanding that when Jericho was destroyed, Israel would spare her family. The spies said her kindness to them would be rewarded. Not only was Rahab rewarded and her family spared, this prostitute was included in the gene pool of the messianic line (see Matt. 1:5).

This is shocking for many—until they realize that David, the king of Israel and an adulterer and murderer, was also part of that heritage. The truth is that all of us are sinners, and so we all were the catalyst that made it necessary for Jesus to come and save us from our own particular sin by giving His life for us. Just like Rahab and David, we all were lost and separated from God. No matter what our sin was, we could know what it meant to have our sin washed whiter than snow.

—*M. K.*

132. Is the modern state of Israel a fulfillment of prophecy?

For any person who believes in God's sovereignty and providence, it is hard not to conclude that the establishment of the state of Israel in 1948 was part of His plan. Even more than providence, it is a fulfillment of Bible prophecy.

First, the Bible predicts that Israel would return to its land in unbelief. Many question the prophetic nature of Israel's return because most Jewish people do not yet believe in Jesus. But biblical prophecy indicates that the Jewish people would only turn to the Messiah after returning to the land of Israel: "For I will take you out of the nations; I will gather you from all the countries and bring you back into your own land. I will sprinkle clean water on you, and you will be clean; I will cleanse you from all your impurities and from all your idols. I will give you a new heart and put a new spirit in you; I will remove from you your heart of stone and give you a heart of flesh" (Ezek. 36:24–26). Note that the national restoration of the Jewish people will precede the spiritual regeneration of Israel.

Second, the Bible predicts that Israel would return in stages. Ezekiel's vision of the valley of dry bones describes a series of events. The bones come to life in stages, first sinews on the bones, then flesh, then skin, and finally, the breath of life (37:6–10). God tells Ezekiel, "These bones are the people of Israel" (v. 11) and their restoration is a picture of the way God will bring them "back to the land of Israel" (v. 12). This is precisely how the Jewish people have returned to their land. Through the different waves of immigration, beginning in 1881 to the present, the Jewish people have returned in stages.

Third, the Bible predicts that Israel would return through persecution. God says, "I will restore them to the land I gave their ancestors" (Jer. 16:15), and He says that He will use "fishermen" and "hunters" (v. 16) to pursue His people back to their land. This metaphor for persecution has been fulfilled in the rebirth of Israel. Historically, the primary motivation for Jews to return to the land of Israel has been anti-Jewish persecution. For more than a hundred years, God has used czarist pogroms, Polish economic discrimination, Nazi genocide, Arab hatred, Soviet repression, and revived European anti-Semitism to drive Jewish people back to their ancient homeland. God uses "fishermen and hunters" to pressure Jewish people back to the land of promise.

Finally, the Bible predicts that Israel would return to set the stage for end-time events. Daniel speaks of a firm covenant between the future world dictator and the Jewish people, which will unleash the final events before Messiah's return (9:27). This prophecy assumes a reborn state of Israel. The Jewish state had to be restored so that the events described by Daniel can take place. Without Israel back in its land, this prediction (and many others) cannot be fulfilled.

Yes, from the biblical evidence it appears that the modern state of Israel is indeed a fulfillment of ancient prophecy, setting the stage for the imminent return of Messiah Jesus.

—*M. R.*

133. What do you think about the claims of some that Noah's ark has been discovered?

All I know about the search for Noah's ark, and the latest claims to have found it, is what I read in the newspaper and/or the internet. Apparently, explorers found some petrified beams high on a mountain in Iran. To the members of the expedition, the beams looked like an ancient shipwreck.

Were they Noah's boat? We don't know. But I do not believe the beams—even if verified by atheistic scientists to be vestiges of Noah's ark—would impress anybody but those of us who are disposed to believe. When Noah was building the ark, nobody paid attention to him; nobody believed it would rain cats and dogs and drown everybody except those who had passage on the boat. See Genesis 7:23; Luke 17:25–27; Hebrews 11:7; 1 Peter 3:20; 2 Peter 2:4–5.

Conceivably, proof that the petrified beams were Noah's boat could convince some that the Bible's story of the great flood is true. But belief in the credibility of the Bible does not necessarily lead to faith in God. Abraham told the rich man who was in Hell that his brothers were not listening to Moses and the prophets, and, therefore, not even their dead brother's reappearance would catch their attention (Luke 16:27–31). In the same way, people who ignore or despise the Word of God will not be moved by scholarly evidence that a pile of sticks near the top of a mountain in Iran is Noah's old boat.

—*D. C.*

134. Do angels really have wings?

It's hard for most of us to imagine angels without wings. Our literature and art and culture portray them with wings. Even our hymns describe wings: "Holy, holy, is what the Angels sing, and I expect to help them make the courts of Heaven ring. But when I sing redemption's story, they will fold their *wings*. For angels never felt the joys that my salvation brings."

But there's not much biblical evidence to support the idea that angels have wings. The angels who appeared to biblical characters usually appeared in human form and were accepted and entertained as men (see Gen. 18:1–15). Perhaps the fact that angels are messengers prompted the thought that they would fly from place to place, but no, there's no biblical proof of wings.

Some suggest, however, that the winged cherubim and seraphim appear to be a part of a higher category of angels. The cherubim over the mercy seat in the Ark of the Covenant were winged beings, as were those mighty creatures who overshadowed the ark in Solomon's temple (1 Kings 6:23–28).

—*M. K.*

135. What is the difference between infallibility and inerrancy, if any?

Both words are critical in any discussion of the reliability of the Bible. Taking them in reverse order, inerrancy means that the Scriptures as originally given by God contain no errors. Because the Bible contains no errors, it is infallible—completely trustworthy as a guide to all our faith and practice.

The claim that the Bible has no errors refers to the original manuscripts, also called "autographs," meaning the Scriptures as written by the men through whom the Holy Spirit spoke (see 2 Tim. 3:16; 2 Peter 1:21). The translations that we have today are not necessarily free from errors such as incorrect translations of a Hebrew or Greek word or typos, for example. Scholars acknowledge that the array of manuscripts that we have from history contain remarkably few errors of this nature, and they have been insignificant when discovered.

Because the Bible is inerrant, it is also infallible. Thus, it is trustworthy. You can rely on it to teach you about God and show you the way to Heaven.

—*D. C.*

136. Was Jonah a historical figure, and does it matter?

Jonah was a historical figure, which is important for the truthfulness of both Old and New Testament Scripture. The Old Testament book of Jonah presents the story as a factual account, and in the New Testament Jesus refers to the historicity of Jonah to describe His coming resurrection and judgment upon the unbelieving generation (Matt. 12:39–41; 16:4; Luke 11:29–32).

The book of Jonah begins with the same historical markers as in other prophetic books, such as the beginnings of Jeremiah, Hosea, Joel, and Zechariah. Fictional accounts do not provide the type of details given in the book of Jonah, such as Jonah's journey to Joppa, his payment of the fare, the conversations among the mariners before they cast lots, the entirety of Jonah's prayer and his specific judgment of idolaters within the prayer, and the length of the city of Nineveh and its population.

The book of Jonah describes miraculous events, actions, and occurrences that are not natural, logical, or traditional happenings. They include a storm increasing in intensity specifically against the sailors, a fish large enough to swallow a man whole being present at the very moment Jonah is in the water during a violent storm at sea, a fish holding Jonah for three days and nights without digesting or suffocating him, the appearance of Jonah in Nineveh by means of a fish, and the raising and withering of a plant within a day.

If we attempt to explain the miraculous happenings as natural events, we deny the supernatural ability of God and the supernatural character of Scripture. God's sovereignty and omnipotence are on display in the book of Jonah, and we should not diminish that by claiming these mighty acts were mere fiction. While we should not expect those with eyes closed to Christ to see the miraculous as true, we should also feel burdened to make the miraculous credible to them. We need supernatural eyes to see the truth.

—*E. C. R.*

137. Should a follower of Christ be concerned about the cultivation of the imagination?

This is a very good question, and I am thrilled that you are raising it. In our North American pulpits, very little preaching appeals to the imagination of the listener. The evangelical imagination is malnourished, frail, and emaciated. Indeed, I would say that the scandal of the evangelical imagination is that there isn't much of an evangelical imagination.

Imagination is a creative capacity. When we read literature we use our imagination: we visit places, meet people, walk where they walked, smell what they smelled, and see what they saw. As people created in the image of God, the imaginative faculty is a part of that image. Since the imagination is a part of the image of God in us, we should be concerned about the cultivation and sanctification of the imagination. Of course, my answer is more theological than exegetical, but in examining Scripture, we must conclude that the cultivation and purification of the imagination is part of renewing the mind (Rom. 12:2). Not only should our thinking be in harmony with God's mind, but our imagination should be going through the process of renewal.

John Bunyan, G. K. Chesterton, and C. S. Lewis serve as examples of Christians who used their sanctified imaginations in the service of Christ. I have some suggestions that may help you cultivate a sanctified imagination: (1) Deepen your prayer life and worship. Ask God to show you His glory. The late Archbishop of Canterbury, William Temple, said, "To worship is . . . to purge the imagination by the beauty of God." Ask the Lord in prayer to show you His beauty, to show you the wonder of His person, and ask Him to purify your imagination with His thrilling glory and indescribable wonder. (2) When you read the Bible, especially the narrative sections of the Old and New Testament, use your imagination. Visit the places and enter the world of the biblical characters in your mind. (3) Read the great imaginative literature of the church like John Bunyan's *Pilgrim's Progress* and C. S. Lewis's The Chronicles of Narnia.

—*W. N.*

138. Does the Bible teach the existence of guardian angels?

A short answer is yes. The catch is that sometimes short answers lead to conclusions that may not be justified. For instance, the idea that every child of God is protected from harm by a personal guardian angel, without a moment of inattention, is clearly mistaken.

On the other hand, angels are indeed assigned guard duty. Everybody is acquainted with Hebrews 1:14: "Are not all angels ministering spirits sent to serve those who will inherit salvation?" The Old Testament speaks frequently of special assignments. See Abraham's assurance to his servant—whom he had sent eastward to find a bride for Isaac—that the Lord would send His angel with him to make the journey a success (Gen. 24:7). That angel was the servant's guide and protector until the journey's end. See also Exodus 33:2 and similar references to the journey to the Promised Land.

The New Testament is equally rich in references to duties performed by angels on behalf of the Lord's servants. Read the account of Peter's escape from jail (Acts 12); you can check a concordance for other references to angels. My favorites relate the story of the angels in white uniforms who rolled away the stone at the tomb, showed the women that the grave was empty, and scared the guards half to death.

I personally do indeed believe in the existence of guardian angels. On unforgettable occasions I have experienced their protection.

—D. C.

139. I am a Christian, but I am troubled by Bible verses that promote slavery; to me, this seem so unfair. Does the Bible promote slavery? How widespread was slavery in the New Testament era?

Unfortunately, in the New Testament era, slavery was entrenched in the culture, and slaves were a substantial part of the Greco-Roman world. Class lines between the rich and the poor were sharp and pronounced. There was virtually no middle class because slaves did most of the work. Some people were born in slavery; authorities condemned others to slavery because of debt or crimes. Some were prisoners of war. The system itself was evil, and was evidence of human sinfulness.

The Bible certainly doesn't promote slavery! In the first century, the gospel reached people of various backgrounds, including slaves and masters. As the church grew and the truth of the gospel was taught, it impacted slave and master relationships. Several passages in the New Testament address these relationships, including the letter to Philemon (Eph. 6:5–9;

Col. 3:22–4:1; 1 Tim. 6:1–2; 1 Peter 2:18–25). Christian slaves and Christian masters needed guidelines about how to function within an oppressive system. Though Scripture did not attack slavery directly by saying "Slavery is morally evil," the implications of the gospel slowly undercut the system. If both slave and master could be brothers and sisters in Christ by believing the truth about Jesus, then the system of slavery could no longer make sense or be justified. In no case do these passages defend slavery as system. The Bible never defends slavery. It is a glaring abuse of Scripture and a misrepresentation of God Himself to say that these texts defend slavery.

—W. N.

140. Not long ago I lost my wife. When I get to Heaven will I know her? Will she recognize me? Does she see us or know what is happening to the family?

When we get to Heaven we're going to know more than we know now. I certainly don't think we'll know less. While we shouldn't be dogmatic, I think it is fair to suggest that yes, we'll know each other and rejoice with each other (1 Cor. 13:12).

As far as what people in Heaven know about our lives on earth, Scripture does not answer this question clearly. However, we have a little material on which to base the belief that she *may* know something. (Note that I say *may* know, not *does* know.) First, Moses and Elijah went from Heaven to the Mount of Transfiguration in order to speak with the Lord about His impending death. They had deeper insights into His mission than did the disciples. Were they the only ones in Heaven with the knowledge? Possibly not.

Second, Revelation 6:9–11 notes the concern of some who were murdered for their faith. They wanted to know when God would avenge their blood. They were not given a complete answer; they were told only to wait, "until the full number of their fellow servants, brothers and sisters, were killed just as they has been." Thus, they were assured that justice would be done—according to God's timetable.

Heaven might not be heavenly if the ransomed of the Lord knew *everything* that happens on earth. On the other hand, everybody in Heaven sees things *from God's perspective*. If He who is Love can cope with the knowledge of tragic events in the families of His people on earth, so can the family members already in Heaven. When all is said, we do not know how much they know about happenings on earth.

— *M. K. and D. C.*

141. I'm a nine-year-old boy. Did Adam have a belly button? My friend says he did not; belly buttons evolved.

Your friend is half-right; Adam did not have a belly button, also known as a navel, as in California navel oranges. Neither did Eve. Only people who are born have navels. Adam and Eve were not born; God created them. But everybody after Adam and Eve are formed naturally in their mother's womb and attached to her by an umbilical cord that keeps them alive and growing. After birth, the cord is cut, and the spot where

it was attached to the baby becomes the "scar" known as the navel. Clearly, belly buttons are not the product of evolution.
—D. C.

142. Does baptism save people?

When I was a young man attending a Baptist church, another young man came to me, concerned and upset because of the name of our church. He declared that he didn't think baptism saved anyone, and he thought the name "Baptist" implied that our church believed that baptism was part of salvation. I explained that the name Baptist derived from the Anabaptists, who believed that baptism was an act of obedience in response to our salvation. Salvation comes when we accept by faith the gift of Christ's work on our behalf to deal with our sin and death. Baptism itself does not save anyone.

Frankly, it certainly would be easier to be saved if the only thing necessary to accomplish salvation was to be immersed in or sprinkled by water. But instead, we have to repent of our sins and place our trust in Jesus (Acts 2:38). Baptism is the public proclamation that we have aligned ourselves with Jesus Christ and have accepted His gospel. It is the demonstration before others that we are choosing to follow Christ.

Today many people are baptized in front of other believers in churches. Some churches do prefer, when possible, to host their baptism services in a public place—a public park with a lake or on a beachfront—so they can offer a testimony to the world of the commitment that believers make to follow Jesus. And for many believers around the world, being baptized in the name of the Father, Son, and Holy Spirit is a confession of faith that could bring alienation and often death.

When we accept Christ, we are saved. We can do nothing to add to what Christ has already done for us. Baptism signifies our identity as redeemed by God, but the act of baptism is not what saves us—all the credit for that goes to Jesus' death, resurrection, and His work as our Great High Priest.

—M. K.

143. Is baptism really necessary? If so, why and how?

Of course it is necessary. Jesus instructed the apostles to baptize those who believed the gospel (Matt. 28:19–20). That instruction (i.e., command) has never been rescinded.

The apostles obeyed the command; they baptized their converts. See Acts 2:40–41; 10:47–48; 16:33; 19:1–5. From the time of the apostles until the present, virtually every denomination of Christians has practiced the rite of baptism.

How should it be done? The baptism of the Ethiopian (Acts 8:36–39) implies immersion. They "went down into the water" and "came up out of the water." The method is determined by its meaning. Romans 6:1–4 seems to refer to baptism as a dramatization of our spiritual union with Christ in his death, burial, and resurrection. If this is indeed its meaning (as I believe it to be), then immersion alone can portray death, burial, and rising again.

In fairness, I must admit that many Bible students disagree. They do not question our union with Christ as set forth in Romans 6; they just move it back a step to the coming of the Holy Spirit, who makes the union a spiritual reality.

Consequently, they sprinkle new believers. Sprinkling illustrates the meaning of baptism as they see it.

—*D. C.*

144. I was in class the other day, and my professor (at a secular university) said that she did not believe in predestination, because if God chose some and did not choose others then that means that those not chosen automatically go to Hell. Can you help me sort through this matter?

This issue holds more complexity and tension than the professor's statement seems to show on the surface. Thoughtful Christians have tried to sort through the doctrines of election and predestination for the last two thousand years! It seems to me that the Scripture teaches three truths about this issue: (1) God the Father chose every follower of Christ to be in Christ before the foundation of the world, predestining them to salvation and full conformity to Christ (Rom. 8:28–30; Eph. 1:3–5). This is a choice and destiny of grace from all eternity, not dependent on any merit within the person chosen.

(2) Christ died on the cross for the entire human family (1 Tim. 2:3–6; 1 John 2:1–2), but each one of us is responsible to believe the gospel, receiving Christ in faith (John 3:16, 5:24; Acts 16:30–31; 2 Peter 3:9). The sovereignty of God in election and predestination does not eliminate our responsibility to trust Christ for salvation.

(3) God has chosen to allow some people to reject His Son and to experience the eternal consequence of that decision.

People are in Hell not so much because God sent them there, but because they chose to go there, rejecting Christ as their personal Lord and Savior (Matt. 25:41–46; John 3:3, 16–21; Rev. 20:11–15).

—W. N.

145. How can I become a Christian?

The word "Christian" has become almost meaningless in our culture. But according to the Bible, it means a person who has trusted in the Lord Jesus Christ and become a genuine follower of Him. So how does someone become a Christian or a genuine follower of Christ?

Becoming a follower of Christ starts with understanding that we have all done wrong things. Although we may call this "making mistakes," the Scriptures call it "sin." Clearly, no person lives up to God's holy standards. That's why the Bible says, "For all have sinned and fall short of the glory of God" (Rom. 3:23). In fact, the Bible says something we all know to be true in our hearts: "there is no one on earth who is righteous, no one who does what is right and never sins" (Eccl. 7:20).

Even more tragic news is that our wrong actions separate us from God. The prophet Isaiah reminded us of this in the Bible when he wrote: "But your iniquities [another word for sin] have separated you from your God; your sins have hidden his face from you, so that he will not hear" (Isa. 59:2). All our wrong actions have alienated us from our Creator because our sins deserve God's judgment.

But the Bible also gives good news. God loves us so much that He became a man and took the punishment for our sins.

171

The Scriptures say, "But God demonstrates his own love for us in this: While we were still sinners, Christ died for us" (Rom. 5:8). Not only did Jesus die to take the punishment we deserve, but God "raised Christ from the dead" (Eph 1:20) proving that His sacrifice was accepted and that His declarations of being God in the flesh were true.

Our response to this good news is simple: we only need to believe in the Lord Jesus Christ, putting our trust in His death and resurrection for us. The Bible says, "Believe in the Lord Jesus, and you will be saved [i.e., forgiven by God]" (Acts 16:31). It also says, "Yet to all who did receive him, to those who believed in his name, he gave the right to become children of God" (John 1:12). In the Bible, to believe means "to trust." We do that all the time—we trust in a doctor, or a friend, or a spouse. When it comes to God, we need to trust in the death of the Lord Jesus on our behalf, that He took the punishment we deserve and then was raised from the dead, proving He really is God. Even as you read this, if you will simply trust Christ, God promises to forgive you and make you His child. And that is how to become a genuine Christian.

—*M. R.*

146. Is confession of sins necessary to be saved?

If you are asking if we must itemize each of our sins and confess them, the answer is no. It would be impossible to remember all our sins in order to confess them. Besides, the Bible teaches that salvation depends on believing the gospel, which requires us to "turn to God in repentance and have faith in our Lord Jesus" (Acts 20:21).

Our English Bibles use the terms *confess* and *confession* in two ways: first, as testifying to the truth of something, such as the proclamation of the gospel (1 Tim. 6:13); second, as acknowledging specific sin, and in particular sins against a fellow human being (James 5:16). These distinctions are easily recognized. The first meaning of confession is what is required of us to receive salvation as the free gift of God—to confess with our mouths the Lord Jesus and believe in our hearts that God has raised Him from the dead (Rom. 10:9, 10). The second meaning refers to reconciliation with an estranged brother or sister.

We do acknowledge that we are sinners in need of Savior. And we do cling to the promise of 1 John 1:9, that our ongoing confession of our sin before the Lord will be met with His forgiveness and restoration. But that does not mean that going through each point on our laundry list of sins will save us, even if such a thing were possible. The point of confession is to acknowledge that Jesus is Lord and that we have faith in Him.

147. Can I really know for certain that I am saved?

This was probably the most frequently asked question by callers to the *Open Line* program, which I hosted for many years on the Moody Radio network. If we could not know for sure that God has saved us, we could have no enjoyment of our salvation.

A key passage that would answer your question is 1 John 5:13: "I write these things to you who believe in the name of the Son of God so that you may know that you have eternal life."

Having read that, go back to verses 11 and 12. You indeed can know that you are saved. I have a more thorough explanation in a book published by Moody Publishers, *How to Know You're Saved.* You can find copies online, or ask at your Christian bookstore or church library.

—*D. C.*

148. Is justification the same in the Old Testament as it is in the New Testament?

Both the Old and New Testaments plainly indicate that we are only justified by the singular act of God and not any other way. It is God, and He alone, who declares us righteous. In the Old Testament, God counted men righteous who lived a life of obedience and faithfulness. They believed God and acted on what they believed. Galatians tells us that Abraham believed God, and his faith was put to his account as righteousness. Romans 4:20–22 says that Abraham "did not waver through unbelief . . . [but] gave glory to God, being fully persuaded that God had power to do what he had promised. That is why 'it was credited to him as righteousness.'"

God manifested Himself to humankind through His Son Jesus Christ, who came to bring eternal life. We're told in John 1:12, "to all who did receive him, to those who believed in his name, he gave the right to become children of God." Verse 14 declares, "The Word became flesh and made his dwelling among us. We have seen his glory, the glory of the one and only Son, who came from the Father, full of grace and truth." The apostle Paul made it clear that while all of humankind died as a result of Adam's sin, the gift of salvation is made available to all through belief in Christ's atoning death on the cross for their sins and His resurrection to eternal life. All the saints, both in the Old Testament and New, are redeemed by Christ's work on Calvary.

—*M. K.*

149. Is it really necessary for laypeople to study the Bible or even read it every day? Isn't a complete knowledge of the Bible the responsibility of the clergy?

The answer to both questions is yes. Knowing the Bible is indeed a primary responsibility of the clergy, but it is not their exclusive responsibility. All God's people need to know the Bible. As the psalmist said, "Your word is a lamp for my feet, and a light on my path" (Ps. 119:105). How else can we find our way at a thousand crossroads in this dark world?

Second Timothy 3:16–17 is the final word on everybody's need to know the Bible, and it lists four ways in which the Bible equips us believers to live righteously. I encourage you to read and study it for yourself.

—*D. C.*

150. Why is God not mentioned in the book of Esther? How can a biblical book not clearly speak of God?

We can't imagine a scholar writing a history of the birth of the United States and omitting George Washington. How much more puzzling that the book of Esther never mentions the name of God, who is central to the entire story! The book tells of a

Jewish girl, Esther, who became the queen of Persia; her cousin, Mordecai, who advised her; and Haman, whose plot to destroy all the Jewish people was ultimately thwarted. Every spring for the past 2,500 years, Jewish people have celebrated the Festival of Purim to remember God's great deliverance (see Esth. 9:27–29). So where is God in the book of Esther? Four possible answers have been given by different scholars.

First, some have said the book is too profane for God to be in it. According to this view, King Xerxes is a sensual despot; Esther is a beautiful, self-promoting manipulator; Mordecai is a rebellious subject who refuses to respect Haman; and the theme of the book is vengeance, making it morally below the Old Testament standard. But this interpretation unacceptably demeans the Word of God and ignores the story of salvation in the book.

A second view is that the scroll of Esther is simply nationalistic propaganda with no spiritual message. The book of Esther is merely a tale of national defense and struggle; as one commentator exclaimed, "God forbid, that God should appear in such a story!" This interpretation minimizes God's determination to protect His chosen people and His success in using someone like Esther to do so.

A third approach views the book of Esther as a picture or an allegory in which God is revealed in the book through the various characters. Mordecai represents the Holy Spirit, the king represents the flesh, Esther represents the redeemed, and Haman represents Satan. But this allegorical approach reduces God's work through these historical characters to nothing more than a parable, ignoring the powerful historical account of the protection of the Jews.

The fourth and best explanation is that the book of Esther is about providence. The name of God is deliberately concealed in order to focus on and reveal His actions. Providence, defined as "God performing a miracle and deciding to remain anonymous," means that God is lovingly guiding all of history with His good purposes and intentions. The book of Esther reveals that the Jewish people had adopted the Persian culture and forgotten their God. The message of this book is that even when Israel forgets God, He always remembers His people. So the name of God is deliberately left out, just as the Jewish people of Persia had left Him out of their lives. It declares that God is actively working even when we do not acknowledge Him.

—*M. R.*

151. Why is the book of Revelation so hard to understand? Is there help anywhere?

Revelation is full of symbols, and symbols—like the meaning of a parable—are sometimes obscure. The symbols found in the book of Revelation first appear elsewhere in the Bible, and without a fairly thorough knowledge of the Bible, a reader is unequipped to understand parts of Revelation. Most of us need the help of an interpreter like Philip. He found an Ethiopian official reading Isaiah and asked him if he understood what he was reading (Acts 8:27–39). The Ethiopian—an educated man—replied, "How can I, unless someone explains it to me?"

The key to understanding the book of Revelation, in addition to knowledge of the Bible as a whole, is to use a good study Bible. You also should find a reliable resource such as the

Moody Bible Commentary. Because the Time Is Near by John MacArthur is also helpful.

—*D. C.*

152. Why do some consider Hannah to be one of the most pious women in the Old Testament?

Hannah, the wife of Elkanah and the mother of Samuel, suffered for years because of her infertility and painful family life (1 Sam. 1:3–7). Her well-intentioned husband misunderstood her (1:8). But Hannah's pain drove her to take her problem to the Lord in prayer (1:10–11). She is the only woman in the Old Testament depicted as praying; she is the only woman whose vow is narrated in Scripture; she is the first person in Scripture to address God as the LORD of hosts (NASB), or LORD Almighty.

After prayer her face was no longer sad (1:18), indicating the Lord's deep work in her soul. She kept her promise to God and dedicated Samuel to the Lord (1:26–28). Samuel became one of the most effective prophets in Israel's history (3:19–21), the one who anointed the first two kings of Israel (10:1; 16:13). Hannah's prayer of rejoicing reaches almost one thousand years in the future and informs Mary's prayer in the New Testament (1 Sam. 2:1–10; Luke 1:46–55). To this day, Hannah stands as a model to be followed.

—*W. N.*

153. Does Hebrews 6:4–6 teach that backsliders lose their salvation?

No, that interpretation has two serious flaws. First, it flies in the face of stories such as the prodigal son and texts such as 1 John 1:9: "If we confess our sins, [God] is faithful and just and will forgive us."

Second, it goes too far. It says that a backslider, having forfeited salvation, has lost it forever. No second chances.

The text is both a warning and an indictment: a warning of the danger and consequence of apostasy, and an indictment of apostates. An ordinary run-of-the-mill backslider must be distinguished from an apostate: the former is someone who has slipped from closeness with God; the second is someone who has renounced God and His Word. The consequence of apostasy is permanent forfeiture of salvation. The indictment (statement of their sin) is that "they are crucifying the Son of God all over again and subjecting him to public disgrace."

Some unbelievers, living among Jews who were Christians, seem to have claimed to be Christians, but then they eventually renounced Jesus and returned to Judaism. Hebrews declares that this apostasy is shameful and cannot be a mark of those who have really trusted Christ to forgive their sins.

—D. C.

154. I often hear the Scripture "Do not touch my anointed ones; do my prophets no harm." What does this mean?

This admonition is found in 1 Chronicles 16:22 and in Psalm 105:15. In the Old Testament many of God's messengers and prophets were definitely at risk because of the words they spoke, both the foretelling and the forthtelling that God had given them to deliver to His people. Jeremiah, known as "the weeping prophet," sorrowed because he knew that in spite of his words of warning, the Lord's people were not going to listen to him and would be judged for their sinfulness.

Also, the warnings of the prophets could result in bodily harm when they preached the word of the Lord. Jeremiah was often brutalized: put in stocks for public ridicule, imprisoned in a well, and taken into Egypt against his will. Elijah had to flee into the desert to escape from the murderous wrath of Queen Jezebel. Prophets faced the possibility of death if they delivered a word from God that a king didn't want to hear. Samuel is just one of the prophets we read about in Hebrews 11:32–38: "Some faced jeers and flogging, and even chains and imprisonment."

Unfortunately, this verse is often used wrongly to refer to pastors today who deserve criticism for their messages and conduct within the church. This verse does not mean that every pastor is exempt from being held accountable for a ministry and lifestyle that do not honor God. What is sad is that often in the church, congregations are being brutalized by harsh pastors who demand authoritarian allegiance. This kind of pastor will try to twist this verse to shield himself from any call to humility and repentance.

—*M. K.*

155. Why do some versions of the Bible leave out Mark 11:26? Is this verse part of Scripture?

In the *New King James Version*, Mark 11:26 says, "But if you do not forgive, neither will your Father in heaven forgive your trespasses." But other translations, including the ESV, NLT, and NIV do not print the verse, and the NASB and HCSB print the verse with brackets and notes, indicating that the textual tradition following the earliest manuscripts of the New Testament does not contain this verse. When the KJV was translated, the earliest manuscripts to which modern translations have access had not yet been discovered.

In the case of Mark 11:26, later scribes and those tasked with copying the Scriptures by hand likely had access to Matthew 6:14–15 and 18:35, which have similar words and concepts. It is likely a copier added the verse in Mark, thinking that they were missing since they appeared in the passage in the gospel of Matthew.

Most scholars agree that the older manuscripts that were copied closer to the time of the original writings of the New Testament are more accurate than those copied during a much later period of history. It is also known that later scribes were more likely to make a reading easier to read than more difficult and more likely to add words than take away words known to be inspired.

Mark 11:26 agrees with the testimony of inspired Scripture in the gospel of Matthew, and in that sense it is not a false or untrue word. But this verse almost certainly was not in the original text of the gospel of Mark, which our contemporary translations indicate with brackets or a note.

—*E. C. R.*

156. Since the devil no longer has power and authority over us, why does the Bible command us to put on the full armor of God?

The Lord's decisive defeat of the devil through the cross does not mean we are no longer involved in spiritual battles and fierce struggles. The Lord Jesus has already won the war, but we are still engaged in spiritual battles against the powers of darkness (Eph. 6:12). Sometimes these battles are fierce. But it is important to note what the text says. It says, "put on the full armor of God, so that you can take your stand against the devil's *schemes*" (Eph. 6:11, italics added).

The text does not say stand firm against the *power* of the devil, but stand firm against the *schemes* of the devil. His power was broken at the cross, but we do have to be prepared to stand against his schemes. These schemes are his diabolical methods, his cunning strategies that he uses to catch us off guard, to tempt us, and to deceive us. Armed, however, with the power and armor of God, we are enabled to stand against the cunning methods of the devil.

—*W. N.*

157. I am puzzled by statistics in Genesis 11:26 and 12:4. When he was 70, Terah became the father of Abraham. Not until Terah died—135 years later at age 205—did Abraham leave Haran (Acts 7:4). Yet Abraham was said to be only 75 at the time (Gen. 12:4). The figures don't compute. Is this an error in the Bible?

No, it is not an error. Genesis 11:26 lists three sons born to Terah after he turned 70. They were not triplets, and they were not listed chronologically. We don't know who came first. The oldest of the three was 135 when his father died. Since Abraham was 75, he was 60 years younger than the firstborn. Between Abraham and his older brother came at least one other sibling who was named and perhaps a dozen or more unnamed brothers and sisters. If there were others, the reason for silence about their names is that their vital statistics were not germane to the story in Genesis.

—D. C.

158. In the Old Testament, a priest had to offer sacrifices for the people, but we know that no one is saved by the sacrifice of bulls and goats. How then were these Old Testament saints saved? We know they had not heard of Jesus.

They were saved by faith in the promises of God, just as we are.

Key passages in understanding the issue are Romans 3:21–26, Galatians 3:6–14, and Hebrews 11. Taken together, they teach (1) that the basis of salvation has always been the death of Christ; (2) the means of salvation has always been faith; (3) the content of saving faith has varied through the ages; and (4) faith that saves calls for obedience.

We find this truth affirmed in the New Testament: "And the scripture was fulfilled that says, 'Abraham believed God, and it was credited to him as righteousness,' and he was called God's friend" (James 2:23). The litany of Old Testament saints in Hebrews 11 reminds us again and again that they were saved by faith. By faith, Abel was commended as righteous; by faith, Enoch was commended as one who pleased God; and by faith, Noah became an heir of righteousness. Sarah, Rahab, Gideon, and Moses were all saved by faith. The chapter ends this stirring roll call of Old Testament heroes by saying, "These were all commended for their faith" (v. 39). They and everyone else listed in Hebrews 11 shared three convictions: God exists, He rewards those who seek Him (v. 6), and genuine faith leads to obedience to God.

Old Testament saints believed that God would fulfill His promise to send a Savior. They believed in God's promise to provide a way for them to dwell with Him forever. Today, we are saved through faith that God has fulfilled His promise to send a Savior. We trust in the person and work of Jesus, who made the final sacrifice for our sins: "For it is by grace you have been saved, through faith—and this is not from yourselves, it is the gift of God—not by works, so that no one can boast" (Eph. 2:8–9).

—*M. K. and D. C.*

159. I have an acquaintance who believes in reincarnation. What does the Bible say?

Other religions, notably Hinduism and Buddhism, teach various versions of reincarnation. But the Bible says, "People are destined to die once, and after that to face judgment" (Heb. 9:27). In other words, people are born once and die once on this earth.

Jesus did teach that we can be born again (see John 3). But the Christian doctrine of spiritual regeneration is very different from the teaching of reincarnation. Reincarnation means an ongoing process of physical rebirth until an individual improves his or her karma enough to leave the physical, material world. Being born again means trusting in the person and work of Jesus, which makes it possible for us to have eternal life with God even after our physical death. We have eternal life not because we can do anything to be good enough to live with God but only because God's love makes it possible (see Eph. 1:1–14).

Some have suggested that Jeremiah 1:5 hints at reincarnation. God says to Jeremiah, "Before I formed you in the womb I knew you, before you were born I set you apart; I appointed you as a prophet to the nations." But this verse is not describing Jeremiah's reincarnation. Instead, it means that even before his birth, Jeremiah was loved by God, who had a plan for his life. Psalm 139 also conveys this truth of God's knowledge and love for us.

—*M. K.*

160. What is the meaning of the Lord's miraculous signs in the gospel of John?

From the many miracles Jesus performed, John selected and recorded seven of them in his gospel. His selection was rooted in evangelistic purposes, which he identifies in John 20:31, and each of the seven signs had a particular significance.

Jesus changed the water into wine, pointing to His power over quality (John 2:1–11). The Lord's healing of the nobleman's son points to His power over distance (John 4:46–54). When the Lord healed the man at the pool of Bethesda, He demonstrated His power over time (John 5:1–9). His feeding of the five thousand demonstrated His power over quantity (John 6:1–13).

The Lord's calming of the sea points to His power over nature (John 6:15–21). Jesus healed the man born blind, pointing to His power over tragedy and misfortune (John 9). And when He raised Lazarus from among the dead, He revealed His power over death (John 11).

What a mighty Savior we know and serve!

—*W. N.*

161. Since the Bible appears to support a pro-life position that requires God to be both the giver and taker of life, what does the Bible have to say about capital punishment? Doesn't the Bible say, "Thou shalt not kill"?

The Scriptures do authorize capital punishment for intentional murder, what is categorized in the US criminal justice system today as first-degree homicide. We see this divine authorization of capital punishment before the Law of Moses was given to Israel, in the days just after the flood: "Whoever sheds human blood, by humans shall their blood be shed; for in the image of God has God made mankind" (Gen. 9:6). Murder is forbidden because of humanity's high status as created in the image of God, and God declared that capital punishment is an appropriate penalty for anyone who intentionally takes the life of another person.

When the Law of Moses was given, Israel was commanded, "Anyone who strikes a person with a fatal blow is to be put to death" (Ex. 21:12). This is also supported in the New Testament, where human governments are granted divine authority to approve those who do good and to punish those who do wrong (see Rom. 13:1–7). Governmental authority can "bear the sword" (Rom. 13:4), a reference to capital punishment.

Some have objected that certain murderers in the Bible were not put to death. For example, Cain killed Abel but was not put to death (Gen. 4:1–16). But the ability and the authority to carry out capital punishment for murder does not mean that Scripture requires it to be implemented in every instance.

Other objections to capital punishment are more philosophical in nature. Some contend that taking the life of a murderer will send that person to Hell. This is a misunderstanding of what determines our eternal destiny. The murderer's sin and depravity separates him from God, not capital punishment. Moreover, some on death row have turned to God for forgiveness, and their sentence hastened repentance.

Others object that capital punishment does not work as a deterrent for other murderers. This may or may not be so, but it certainly is a deterrent for that particular murderer not to kill again.

Finally, some object that capital punishment is inhumane, not treating the murderer with human dignity. Actually, the opposite is true. Too often people attempt to offer excuses to explain their choice to end the life of someone else. But tolerating these excuses for murder actually minimizes human dignity. A government's use of capital punishment says to the murderer, "You, as a person made in the image of God, sought to destroy that image in another person. Therefore, you must be punished." God has ordained human governments to carry out capital punishment not as a means of demeaning or diminishing humanity, but because it upholds the dignity of humanity made in the image of God.

—*M. R.*

162. My priest says that the Roman Catholic Church is the "pillar and foundation of the truth." Do you agree?

The phrase "the pillar and foundation of the truth" is found in 1 Timothy 3:15. The preceding verse sets forth Paul's objective in writing to Timothy. He lays out "how people ought to conduct themselves in God's household, which is the church of the living God, the pillar and foundation of the truth." The context is a local church, not an organization or denomination. At the time, Timothy was dealing with problems in the church in Ephesus.

The New Testament has two concepts of "the church": first is all believers, also called "the church universal," the body of Christ, and the bride of Christ. The second concept is far more commonly used, which is local gatherings of Christians. With one exception (Ephesians), Paul's epistles to churches are directed to local churches and deal with issues in those specific churches. The Roman Catholic Church claims to be the only universal church and, therefore, the arbiter of truth. On biblical and historical grounds, Protestants reject that claim. Local churches, and indeed the entire body of Christ, should be the pillar and support of the truth, but the legitimacy of a particular denomination's claim is determined only by its adherence to the truth that was "once for all entrusted to God's holy people" (Jude 3).

The debate is about authority. The Roman church contends that its traditions and teachings are as authoritative as Scripture. Protestants insist on the supremacy of Scripture and believe that Roman Catholic teaching deviates from Scripture in critical areas.

—D. C.

163. I remember when I was a kid and I was acting like kids sometimes do that my mother would say, "Why don't you grow up?" But in Luke 18, Jesus told His disciples that they needed to be like little children. What did He mean?

The disciples, after hearing Jesus speaking of His impending death on the cross, began shortly thereafter to argue among themselves about who would be the greatest. It was as if they didn't fully understand what He was telling them and continued to focus on their future stake in His soon-to-come kingdom. No wonder they were shattered after He was crucified and buried! He was talking about His death, and they continued arguing about who was the greatest.

Jesus knew what they were thinking and took a child and brought him close and sat him on His lap. He said, "Anyone who will not receive the kingdom of God like a little child will never enter it" (Luke 18:17). In that culture, children had no status and absolutely no power. They were the lowest rungs of the ladder, often equated with slaves. Jesus was trying to tell His disciples that worldly measures of success were not the key to entering His kingdom; rather, humility and simplicity are more valued in the spiritual realm.

Often as church members we have that same tension among ourselves as the disciples did—always trying to promote ourselves, our positions, and our agenda. We still need to hear Jesus' message to grow up spiritually—and be like little children.

164. (From Phoebe H., age 6) How do angels put on their clothes while having wings on their backs?

The first possible explanation is that not all angels have wings. Angels who make themselves visible on earth look like men with arms and legs. When the women went to the grave of Jesus, "Suddenly two men in clothes that gleamed like lightning stood beside them" (Luke 24:4). It's likely that angels don't wear clothes like ours—they may just be covered with light. Or, their wings may be detachable, like the zippered hoods on a winter parka. Detachable wings would be handy for angels.

—D. C.

165. What is the meaning of the "days" of creation? Are we to understand the days of Genesis 1 as literal 24-hour periods?

Godly followers of Christ throughout church history have understood the days of Genesis 1 in different ways. But one's position on this issue should not be a litmus test of orthodoxy and evangelical commitment.

Many Bible believers maintain that the "days" are actually "ages," long periods of time that might range from years to even millions of years. And it is possible for the word "day" to mean a period of time and not a 24-hour revolution around the sun. For example, in Genesis 2:4, the entire six-day period of creation is literally called the "day" or "when the LORD God made the earth and heavens." Also, the prophets use the phrase "the day of the LORD" to describe the entire period of the end times.

But one of several problems in adopting this "day-age" view is that death only entered the world with Adam and Eve's sin (Gen. 2:17; 3:3). A "day-age" interpretation would require death in each of the ages, so that the fittest could survive and evolve, before Adam and Eve's fall. It would be surprising for fossils, which indicate dead animals, to exist before the fall of humanity.

Alternatively, it is possible to interpret the creation account as referring to six 24-hour days. This would likely mean that the earth is relatively young. The 24-hour day interpretation is supported by the simplest, most normal reading of the passage. The text does not indicate that Moses was referring to an age when he used the word "day." Moreover, the repetition of the phrase, "and there was evening, and there was morning" (Gen.

1:5, 8, 13, 19, 23, 31) seems to refer to a 24-hour period.

This interpretation seems to contradict the evidence of an old earth as well as the fossil record. Yet, it is not impossible to hold to a young earth for two reasons. First, God may have created the earth with apparent age. Just as Adam and Eve did not look like infants but adults when they were created, so God could very well have created the earth with seeming age.

Second, the fossil record could be explained by a vast, worldwide catastrophe rather than a long period of time. For example, when Mount St. Helens erupted in 1980, a huge forest was cast into Spirit Lake below. The trees became water-logged and floated to the bottom. Since the roots had the most water, the trees settled in an upright fashion. Thirty-five years after the eruption, a petrified forest is now at the bottom of the lake. Any person seeing it would assume that it took millions of years. But it was caused by a catastrophe in 1980.

Whichever view one chooses to explain the word "day," what is most important is to recognize God as the Creator of the world in His infinite power and wisdom. It is through the Lord Jesus the Messiah that "all things were created: things in heaven and on earth, visible and invisible . . . all things have been created through him and for him" (Col. 1:16). We must bow before the Lord Jesus, our Creator and Redeemer.

—*M. R. and W. N.*

166. What is the meaning of "handed over to Satan" in 1 Timothy 1:20? Does this indicate hopelessness instead of faith that God would change these people? Or are they really "evil" people?

In this passage Paul is charging Timothy to engage in spiritual warfare, to fight the good fight. The rules of engagement in spiritual warfare include trusting in God and maintaining a good conscience. Some in the church, however, rejected these principles by deliberately and willfully disobeying the Word of God.

Silencing the voice of conscience in order to pursue our own self-centered path has devastating consequences. Paul employs the imagery of a shipwreck (the breaking of a ship into pieces) to graphically describe what happens to one who deliberately disobeys God, violating the gift of a good conscience as Alexander and Hymenaeus did. In silencing their conscience, these two embraced false teaching and began to spread it among believers. In fact, they "shipwrecked" the faith of others (1 Tim. 1:19 NLT).

But even after a shipwreck, not all hope is lost. Paul, and by implication the local church involved, handed these two over to Satan so that they would be taught not to blaspheme. Instead of being a sign of hopelessness, the act is really a sign of hope. The act of turning them over to Satan was a disciplinary measure designed to bring them to repentance. Today we call such a disciplinary measure excommunication. Biblically, excommunication is the last and final resort in a series of disciplinary measures. Church discipline is a process (Matt. 18:15–17). As the final stage in a disciplinary process, excommunication is implemented when a professed Christian refuses to repent of their sin and turn from their evil ways. Keep in mind that this measure was always a last resort, reserved for unrepentant people in the church fellowship. As an act of "tough love," the local church removes the unrepentant person from the fellowship of the local congregation. As a result, the person no longer experiences the help of Christians nor the full protection of God.

The implication is that outside of the local church is the realm of Satan. Outside of the fellowship of believers, the person may be exposed to satanic and demonic attack without access to the full resources of protection in Christ. God permits the person to be exposed to satanic assaults that he would not normally be exposed to while in fellowship in the local church. God, however, is still in control, even using the malicious attacks of Satan to bring a person to repentance. Paul was hoping that being outside of the local church and God's protection and under the oppression of the evil one, these men would learn not to propagate false doctrine in the church. Hopefully, having learned their lesson, these men would be restored to church fellowship.

Church discipline is for the good of God's people, and the aim is always redemptive and remedial. Church discipline should always be exercised in love and meekness with the restoration of the erring person in mind (1 Cor. 5:1–13; Gal. 6:1–2; 2 Thess. 3:14).

—*W. N.*

167. It used to be that when a person died, friends went to the funeral parlor for the viewing. These days, many people say they went to a wake. Is that word biblical?

Neither term is found in the Bible. The words refer to essentially the same thing, yet they are different, too. *Wake* is a specific term for an all-night vigil over a corpse. It has its roots in the ancient, pagan notion that the soul may return to its body, or that something equally spooky may happen. Christians who dislike the word *wake* often use the term *viewing*. They do not keep watch over a corpse. Instead, they visit the place where the body is kept before the burial in order to support bereaved friends. If the body is displayed, as when the coffin is open, they "view" it. They take a last look at the remains of a person they knew and loved in life.

In modern America, not many people stay up all night keeping vigil over a corpse. Many of those who use the term *wake* mean the same thing as those who say *viewing*. Frequently, words drift from their original meaning, and often people continue to use a word without knowing its former denotation. A better term than either of those two words is *visitation*, that is, to visit the bereaved family and try to share their sorrow.

Funerals described in the Bible were marked by simplicity, and common to all was the presence of mourners who grieved before the burial. Check this in Mark 5:21–40; Acts 8:2; and Acts 9:36–42. For most of them, their presence there was a *visitation*.

—D. C.

168. The Bible says a snake talked with Eve. Did other animals in the garden of Eden also know how to talk?

Maybe. The snake was "more crafty than any of the wild animals the LORD God had made" (Gen. 3:1). This does not preclude the possibility that other animals talked. It implies that for Satan's purposes the serpent was the shrewdest creature.

Eve seems not to have been startled by a talking snake. Her willingness to dialog with the snake implies that she expected snakes, and perhaps other animals, to know how to talk.

Much later in human history, the Lord caused Balaam's donkey to speak. The passage is hilarious, as Balaam stands shouting threats at the animal and then answers quietly when the beast reasons with him (Num. 22:21–30). In the millennium, when wild animals revert to their original state ("the wolf will live with the lamb" [Isa. 11:6]), we shall know what the original models could do.

—D. C.

169. The story of Balaam in Numbers 22–24 puzzles me. Are we expected to take literally the conversation between Balaam and his donkey?

Certainly, including the humor of the situation. The spectacle of a man shouting at an animal would not surprise us. But Balaam's heated two-way conversation with the beast was surely hilarious. Yet there is no reason for not believing that it happened as Scripture says it happened. No less remarkable than God's ability to use a donkey's vocal cords was His use of the pagan prophet to make predictions about Israel that were to him, Balaam, very hateful indeed.

The story entered into Israel's collective memory (see Num. 31:8, 15–16; Deut. 23:3–6; Josh. 13:22; 24:9–10; Neh. 13:1–3; Micah 6:5; 2 Peter 2:15–16; Jude 11; Rev. 2:14). Balaam had to be silenced, and God silenced him by putting words in the mouth of a beast without speech. It was as if God wanted Balaam to know that he and his donkey were on the same intellectual level.

—R. d.

170. I am a new Christian and am reading through the Bible. But I got bogged down in the book of Leviticus. The repetitious descriptions of offerings are unbelievably boring. Yet my pastor assures us that boring, seemingly pointless chapters are also inspired by the Holy Spirit. Is there something wrong with me?

No, you are quite normal. I knew a teenager who resolved to read the Bible from Genesis to Revelation in his morning devotions. Two or three months later, he expressed the same complaint as yours. For him, Leviticus had become a slough of despond. I told him that he was misusing Leviticus. It was not written for purely devotional purposes. Until you have become a Bible student with some experience, fly through Leviticus for an idea of its contents. Later, you can return to it without pain.

Detailed study of many parts of the Old Testament is possible only to the extent that we have a grasp of the whole Bible.

—D. C.

171. Why was Elisha angry with Jehoash for striking the ground three times instead of five or six times (2 Kings 13:14–24)?

Elisha was using the bow and arrow as a teaching tool. It seems that after the shooting of the first arrow, additional arrows still remained. Elisha instructed Jehoash to take those arrows and strike them against the ground. Jehoash at this point was aware of the symbolic significance of these instructions and the faith demanded in their execution—Elisha had already prophesied a victory over Aram after he shot the first arrow. He struck the ground three times, but Elisha's response indicates that he left additional arrows unused.

The unused arrows indicated Jehoash's belief that God's actions on his behalf were limited. He did not trust the Lord to do what was represented in the symbolic action of striking all the arrows on the ground. Consequently, the man of God became angry at Jehoash because of his lack of confidence in the Lord. Note the text does not say *Elisha* was angry with Jehoash; it says *the man of God* was angry with Jehoash. As the man of God, Elisha represented the mind of God. His anger was an expression of God's displeasure with King Jehoash's lack of faith.

—*W. N.*

172. Have all the prophecies about the Lord's coming been fulfilled? Are we living in the end times? How close are we?

Yes, we are living in the end times! But if you use the expression "end times" to mean a year or two, more or less, before the Lord returns, my answer is, I don't know when the Lord will come. Neither does anybody else.

Soon after the Jesus' ascension to Heaven, in his first public sermon the apostle Peter explained the phenomenon of tongues as a fulfillment of a prophecy of Joel: "In the last days, God says, I will pour out my Spirit on all people" (Acts 2:17). Later the apostle John said, "Dear children, this is the last hour"

(1 John 2:18). If saints living about two thousand years ago were in the last hour, so are we.

You asked about fulfillment of prophecy. Well, if all the prophecies about the Lord's coming were fulfilled, He would be here, or at least be on the way. How close is He? The answer is in Romans 13:11–12: "The hour has already come for you to wake up from your slumber, because our salvation is nearer now than when we first believed. The night is nearly over; the day is almost here."

That is as close as I can safely predict: nearer than when we first believed. Peter reminds us: "With the Lord a day is like a thousand years, and a thousand years are like a day" (2 Peter 3:8).

—D. C.

173. A friend at work insists that the book of Revelation predicts the appearance of astronauts and spaceships. Is he right?

No. It's one more illustration that many theologically un-sophisticated people find whatever they want in the book of Revelation.

—D. C.

174. Proverbs 22:6 says, "Train up a child in the way he should go, even when he is old he will not depart from it" (NASB). Is that a promise that my children will become Christians?

I wish it were, but I don't think it is. The book of Proverbs is a collection of proverbs, not promises. A proverb is, by definition, "a brief popular maxim." It is true, generally speaking, that how we rear our children determines how they will conduct themselves when they are grown. But there are exceptions to everything, and Proverbs 22:6 has its exceptions—unless every prodigal child is explained as the result of bad training. That would be unfair to the parents of children who did not follow them in the faith. Samuel was a great prophet who named his sons, Joel (Jehovah is God) and Abijah (my father is Jehovah), indicating his desire to bring them up in the faith. But, the Bible says, "his sons did not follow his ways" (1 Sam. 8:3).

If we make Proverbs 22:6 a promise, we bring it into conflict with other issues, such as determining just what is meant by "the way they should go." Is it the same for every child?

—D. C.

175. Why is there such an emphasis in the Scripture for making a joyful noise unto the Lord?

I had a pastor who recognized his deficiency in musical talent and yet never tired of "singing with great gusto"—which some would call "great noise." I loved his enthusiasm. In his monotone voice he triumphantly made his way through many a great hymn and praise song. I believe God was greatly honored by his singing.

I think so much of Christianity is about our hearts and our emotions, not just what we know in our head. Music has a way of connecting truth with the deepest places in our hearts. It's one of the reasons D. L. Moody believed that music should be part of his evangelistic campaigns, and he employed Ira Sankey as his esteemed song leader and choir director. Psalm 33:3 cheers us on to sing new songs to God and shout for joy. The natural response of a sensitive heart is praise.

—*M. K.*

176. How did King Saul die? First Samuel 31:4 says that he "took his own sword and fell on it." But the next chapter (2 Sam. 1:1–16) continues the story and recounts the tale of an Amalekite who reported to King David that he himself had killed Saul. What really happened? Was one of the writers of the Bible confused?

No, the writer was not confused. The account in 1 Samuel 31 focuses on the essentials of the story: that Israel was defeated in battle with the Philistines, that Saul's three sons were slain, and that Saul himself was seriously wounded by enemy archers. Saul knew that he could not survive, and, fearing torture at the hands of the Philistines, he jumped on his sword, ending his own life.

Along came an Amalekite, probably to strip the bodies of

the dead (1 Sam. 31:8). Thinking that he was lucky in finding Saul, he finished him off. Another reasonable possibility is that, finding Saul already dead, the Amalekite concocted the story in order to impress David the next day.

The story told by the Amalekite and David's reaction is the substance of the second account. The story does have the ring of truth, and David seems to have believed the Amalekite. But the Amalekite didn't anticipate David's anger for slaying the Lord's anointed. On earlier occasions, when he himself had ample opportunity to kill Saul, David had refused to do so. In any case, both the account in 1 Samuel 31 and the account in 2 Samuel 1 are true.

—*D. C.*

177. If David was a man after God's own heart, how do we explain his behavior in 2 Samuel 11 and 12?

David was a man after God's own heart (1 Sam. 13:14; Acts 13:22), and he was one of the godliest men who breathed earth's air. Next to Moses, no other person in the Old Testament captured the heart and imagination of Israel like David. In 1 and 2 Samuel, nearly forty chapters are devoted to David's life. David was also a poet who composed numerous divinely inspired psalms, impacting and shaping the worship of ancient Israel and the church.

Yet, in 2 Samuel 11 and 12 we encounter another side of David. There David yielded to temptation and did more than commit adultery; he abused his power and took Bathsheba like she was a spoil in battle (2 Sam. 11:4). The one-night stand took an unexpected turn—Bathsheba conceived a child. In order to cover his immoral tracks, David eventually had Bathsheba's husband killed, and then David took Bathsheba to be his wife. David's descent into the pit of sexual abuse, adultery, and murder was a very dark and insane time in his life. But we must remember that sometimes even a godly person can make a terrible choice. We must be vigilant and watchful lest we find ourselves making the same kind of sinful decisions. Like David, the only appropriate response is full confession and repentance before God (2 Sam. 12:13; Psalm 51).

—W. N.

178. Are the Jewish people still God's chosen people? Since most Jewish people don't believe in Jesus, haven't Christians become the chosen people?

This question assumes that the church is the new people of God and that the Jewish people are has-beens in the plan of God. To understand the status of Jewish people who do not believe in Jesus, it is necessary to examine Romans 11:28–29.

Romans 11:28 asserts, "As far as the gospel is concerned, they [the Jews] are enemies for your sake." This does not mean that Jewish people are enemies of God or Christians; rather, it refers to their opposition to the gospel. Except for a remnant of Jewish people who have become followers of Jesus (see Rom. 11:1–6), tragically, most Jewish people do not believe in Jesus and reject the good news that Jesus is the Redeemer of Israel. Despite this, however, Jewish people continue to have a special status as God's people. This unique national identity (which is different than their spiritual status) has three aspects.

First, Jewish people remain God's chosen nation. Romans 11:28 continues: "but as far as election is concerned, they are loved on account of the patriarchs." The word election means "chosenness." This refers to God's choice of Abraham, Isaac, and Jacob and their physical descendants to be the people through whom God would make His name known throughout the earth.

One might ask: Aren't believers in Jesus chosen? Yes—Ephesians 1:4 says that believers were chosen before the foundation of the world. But that refers to God's spiritual choice for salvation, not God's national choice of Israel. The Jewish people are still God's chosen people.

Second, the Jewish people remain God's beloved nation. They are loved not because of anything intrinsic in themselves but because of God's commitment to the patriarchs. God loves Gentiles, too—John 3:16 says God loved the world. But God has a special love for the Jewish people, just as I care about children but I have a special love for my sons.

Third, Jewish people retain God's unbreakable promises. Romans 11:29 says that God's gifts and calling to the Jewish people are irrevocable, including the gifts mentioned in Romans 9:4–5 (adoption to sonship, the glory, the covenants—including the land covenant—the law, temple worship, promises of the Abrahamic covenant, and Jesus the Messiah of Israel). Every promise that God made to Israel still belongs to the people of Israel. One day, when the nation turns in faith to Jesus (cf. Rom. 11:26), God will fulfill every one of them.

—*M. R.*

179. In the New Testament, God elevates women to a place of honor, unlike the culture in those days. But in the Old Testament, God seems okay with polygamy and concubines. Why is that?

You are correct that the New Testament honors women in a way that was uncommon in the ancient Greco-Roman world. In his book *How Christianity Changed the World*, Alvin Schmidt notes that in ancient Greece, women had the social status of slaves. They were not allowed to speak in public, and girls were not allowed to attend school. Women were considered inferior to men, and poets even equated them with evil.

The Romans didn't treat women any better. They considered a wife to be the property of her husband and granted him complete control over her and everything she owned.

In contrast, Jesus treated women with respect, and two of His closest friends were Mary and Martha. Rather than discouraging women from learning, Jesus encouraged Mary to sit at His feet and listen to His teaching (Luke 10:38–42). He also violated cultural norms when He started a conversation with a Samaritan woman in public. Likewise, the apostle Paul commanded husbands to love their wives "just as Christ loved the church and gave himself up for her" (Eph. 5:25)—a radical idea in the ancient world.

Certainly, the value God places on women in the New Testament seems inconsistent with the Old Testament practice of polygamy. It also seems inconsistent with Genesis 1 and 2, where God creates male and female in His image and the two become one flesh (Gen. 2:24), intended to reflect Trinitarian life and love.

Some believe polygamy is the result of the curse God placed on the woman after the fall: "Your desire will be for your husband, and he will rule over you" (Gen. 3:16). Sin perverted the relationship between men and women, so it's not surprising that men began to take multiple wives and treat those wives as property.

They also note that Jesus, after His resurrection, appeared first to women, perhaps symbolizing a reverse of the curse. After the resurrection, polygamy is not mentioned in the Bible, and the one-flesh union is revealed to have even more significance. As Paul notes in Ephesians 5:31–32, it signifies a "profound mystery": Christ's relationship to the church.

Scripture always depicts polygamy as causing problems. It seems to be something God temporarily permitted, but (like divorce) only because of the hardness of men's hearts (see Matt. 19:8).

—*J. R.*

180. Will the heavens and earth truly pass away as Christ said?

In God's Word, we often find the words *heaven* or *the heavens* in different contexts. When we speak of the heavens it often has to do with the eternal or spiritual world. But the words include the material stars and space above. Jesus often spoke of the "kingdom of heaven," that eternal place, but we often refer to the "heavens" when we speak of the stars. There is no question that at a point in time all that is material in the galaxies, including this planet, will experience a change or transformation, but Scripture says that in God's divine plan, He will bring "a new heaven and a new earth" where He will abide with His people forever (2 Peter 3:13; Rev. 21:1).

—*M. K.*

181. What is meant by the command to keep the Sabbath day holy? And why isn't it included in the New Testament?

To keep the day "holy" is to observe the day according to God's instructions. The central idea is rest from labor, as specified in Deuteronomy 5:12–15.

In the Deuteronomic account of the Ten Commandments, the Lord reminds the people that they had been slaves in Egypt and that He had brought them out of Egypt. That is why He now commands them to observe the Sabbath. The weekly rest would remind them of a time when they could not rest, because they were slaves.

The link between slavery in Egypt and the Sabbath is reiterated in Ezekiel 20:5–12: "On the day I chose Israel . . . [the Lord says] I gave them my Sabbaths as a sign between us, so they would know that I the LORD made them holy." The Sabbath was something that identified the Jewish people, which explains in part its absence in New Testament instructions to Christians, who are both Gentiles and Jews (see Col. 2:16–17).

—*D. C.*

182. If, as the Bible says, the people of Israel marched around Jericho seven days

in a row, one of those days must have been the Sabbath. But they weren't allowed to work on the Sabbath. So how shall we understand this?

The story is told in Joshua 6. For six days the people marched around Jericho in a ghostly silence broken only by the shuffling of feet. The silent ranks probably terrified the inhabitants of Jericho. On the seventh day, which commentators identify as the Sabbath, the Israelites circled the city seven times. When they had completed seven laps, priests blew their trumpets and Joshua bellowed, "Shout!"

Obviously, on that day the Sabbath was not observed legalistically, as it was under the scribes and Pharisees during the life of Christ. But even they made exceptions to their own innumerable rulings, as Jesus reminded them. If a sheep fell into a pit on the Sabbath, the owner would surely pull it out, Jesus said, approvingly. He added that, "It is lawful to do good on the Sabbath" (Matt. 12:9–14). To rescue a sheep in trouble was to do good and, therefore, it was permissible on the Sabbath. And, since the Lord Himself ordered the march around Jericho on a Sabbath, that also was good. Furthermore, the fact that God sent the walls of Jericho tumbling on the Sabbath gave special significance to the victory.

—*D. C.*

183. When I was growing up, I was taught that Sunday was a day of rest, a time when one did very little. I couldn't play outside, do homework, or do anything much but

stay in the house and read, preferably a Christian book. So I came to dread the day. Today things seem to have gone to the opposite extreme. Christians play sports, shop, go to movies, and do almost anything they choose. How should we think about what we used to call "the Lord's Day"?

I, too, grew up in the generation when some Christians limited activities between Sunday services. Years later, I watched the great change in Christians' attitudes toward Sunday, a day now often treated casually as a "day off," but not necessarily as a day of rest belonging to the Lord.

I have been reading *The Radical Pursuit of Rest* by John Koessler, as fresh and wise a book as anything I've seen on the subject. He writes that when he was young, he "came to see Sunday as a day off like Saturday but without the enthusiasm," not an optimal way to view the day. He notes that today, "Our notion of rest has become commingled with play . . . as arduous as our work." After giving the Sabbath's history, he suggests a new way of looking at the issue: "We practice Sabbath as a discipline by introducing a different rhythm into our schedule . . . abstain[ing] from our ordinary and necessary work" in order "to create an atmosphere that will allow space for God." This is an undistracted time. Koessler concludes, "Rest is ultimately a person"—Jesus, who wants to refresh our spirits. Creating a different rhythm could include a variety of mental, physical, and spiritual pleasures if we used this time to form new habits: fasting from media to be less compulsive, reading well, sitting quietly, listening to music, visiting with friends and family, and enjoying the outdoors, one of God's great and restorative gifts to us. In this way, we find delight not dread in treasuring the Lord's Day as a time to rest.

—*R. d.*

184. Seventh-Day Adventists say the Sabbath is Saturday, and that is when they go to church. Are they right? When is the Sabbath?

The Sabbath (cf. Hebrew: *Shabbat*) is the seventh day of the week. The fourth commandment sets it aside as a day of rest and as a sign between God and Israel (Ex. 20:8–11; 31:16–17). Sunday is the first day of the week and is not to be confused with the seventh. Your Seventh-Day Adventist friends who say the Sabbath is Saturday are right. But whether Saturday, not Sunday, is the preferable day to go to church is another question.

—*D. C.*

185. I have heard it said that the Bible doesn't really address the issue of abortion at all. In fact, some people have told me that Exodus 21:22 proves that the Bible does not equate a fetus with fully human life. How would you respond?

There are many good reasons to support a pro-life position regarding preborn babies. Beyond the moral, legal, ethical, and medical evidence for life in the womb, this answer will just focus on four biblical reasons to support the pro-life position and oppose abortion.

First, God is at work as the designer of life in the womb. In Psalm 139:13–16, the psalmist maintains that God formed him in the womb, including his immaterial, spiritual aspect. God's fearful and wonderful creation included ordaining all the days of the preborn baby's life. Clearly, the psalmist recognized that God was forming life while a child was yet in the womb.

Second, God sets people apart for service to Him from the womb. God told the prophet Jeremiah, "Before I formed you in the womb I knew you, before you were born I set you apart; I appointed you as a prophet to the nations" (Jer. 1:5). God sees the totality of a person's life and has plans for a baby even before formation in the womb. Paul described his call from God as an apostle as ordained from the time he was in his "mother's womb" (Gal. 1:15). How could Jeremiah and Paul be appointed to service if they were not yet fully alive? A calling from God in the womb indicates life in the womb.

Third, God is at work spiritually in an unborn child. For example, the angel Gabriel revealed to Zechariah that his son, John the Baptist, would "be filled with the Holy Spirit even before he is born" (Luke 1:15). And indeed, John had not yet been born when he first responded to the presence of the Messiah Jesus, who was Himself still in the womb: "When Elizabeth heard Mary's greeting, the baby leaped in her womb" (Luke 1:41).

Fourth, and just as importantly, God cares as much for the life of a preborn child as He does for any other life. Some use Exodus 21:22 to maintain that a preborn baby is considered less valuable than a fully born baby. The verse states, "If people are fighting and hit a pregnant woman and she gives birth prematurely but there is no serious injury, the offender must be fined whatever the woman's husband demands and the court allows." Some versions of the Bible translate "she gives birth prematurely" as "she has a miscarriage." Abortion proponents therefore argue that since capital punishment isn't required for the life of the baby, then God did not consider an unborn baby as fully alive. This would be a strong argument—if it were not based on a mistranslation. The Hebrew word here literally means "to go out." So if a man strikes a pregnant woman and the child comes out—in other words, a premature birth—the offender still has to pay a penalty. This translation shows that God is concerned for the rights of preborn children and is in no way a justification for considering a baby in the womb as less than a human being. The Scriptures are clear that preborn babies are truly human life. Therefore, believers must use all their influence to defend those lives.

—*M. R.*

186. I often hear preachers and teachers of the Word talk about the importance of reading the Bible. I believe this and have experienced its life-giving reality in my life. I often feel a kind of dullness creeping over me, however, when I go to open it. Or, I just read mechanically without feeling anything and without remembering what I've read. Sometimes I even feel like I've heard it all before. I'm not living in any active disobedience to the Lord, so this is discouraging. What can I do?

I think many Christians understand this feeling. Many of us today have extensive exposure to Bible teaching. We have an explosion of television and Christian radio programs, conferences, live streaming on the internet, and podcast availability—not to mention actually attending church and Bible study in person. As a result, we are almost over-taught, and our hunger becomes dulled through familiarity and swallowing truth whole without digesting it carefully. And not all the teaching is handled with imagination and dimension; sometimes it can be unadorned truth unintentionally thrown at us, numbing our spirits.

As Alan Jones once wrote, "For many the Christian story no longer bears the mystery. . . . The Christian way of looking at, interpreting, understanding the world has lost its power, its fragrance. It has become sterile, lost behind a mountain of custom, habit. . . . There are precious few living characters in its half-forgotten and emaciated plot."

We cannot confuse listening to Bible teaching with lively, personal interaction with the living Word of God. Yes, there will be dry times when we must continue the habit of reading anyway. However, we must also bring attention to the text, as I said, lively attention. It can be surprisingly moving, maddening, and stunning to look at Scripture anew, as a story, a drama, and God's sovereign work in the lives of flawed individuals. Reading a different version, looking up things you don't know in a good Bible handbook, using maps, thinking about conversations, engaging with the characters' vices and virtues, and seeing God's discipline and mercy are a few ways that you can recover the vitality of Scripture in your life and whet your hunger for it.

—R. d.

187. I've always believed that we are saved by grace not works, but Jesus' instruction to the rich young ruler is confusing. The ruler asks, "What do I have to do to inherit eternal life?" Jesus says, ". . . love your neighbor as yourself." What does Jesus mean?

The Lord Jesus was not saying that keeping the commandments and loving your neighbor would save you, no matter what some people infer from this account, told in Matthew 19:16–22 and Mark 10:17–22. Jesus reviewed the commandments, in effect asking him, "Can you meet the requirements of being good?" The man answered that he had kept all the commandments. Mark's telling of this incident adds that "Jesus looked at him and loved him" (v. 21). Jesus told him that keeping the law includes loving others as well—and that was something this man had never demonstrated in his obedience to God. When Jesus challenged the rich young man to give away all that he had, he went away sad because he had a lot. But even if he could keep all the law and love others it would never be enough. Salvation and eternal life come only from belief in Jesus Christ the Son of God.

—*M. K.*

188. What is the best English version of the Bible?

It is easier for me to name the worst version, or versions, than the best. A few versions are very poor, but *many* are quite good. Serious Bible students have different preferences, depending—to a certain extent—on their choice of philosophies governing translation. Some Bible students like a word-for-word translation. Others prefer a "dynamic equivalent" approach to translation. Perfect word-for-word translations are not possible, of course. Languages are different. Latin languages are wordy; to translate 100 pages of an ordinary book in English takes about 120 pages in Spanish or Portuguese. Still, word-for-word translations stick close to the original text, and many scholars consider them more reliable than other versions. The NASB and ESV are fine examples of this approach.

"Dynamic equivalent" means an attempt to capture the thought of a sentence or paragraph. The New Living Translation excels at this. Its translators did not count words. They gave us the English equivalent of what the writers of the Bible said, or seemed to have intended to say. It is pleasant reading. The NIV uses a combination of both approaches to translation.

Find the version that suits your needs, and, if you can afford it, buy two or more versions. I read several in turn without trying to decide which is best. As a missionary familiar with some of the problems in Bible translation, I can assure you that few if any translations on the mission field can match for accuracy or beauty any of a dozen English language versions. So find a version you like and pay no attention to critics who complain about it.

—D. C.

189. I have been enjoying the Scriptures in the recently published narrative, The Voice. Can this type of paraphrasing be a

single source, or should it be balanced with more traditional translations?

The short answer is that while a paraphrase, carefully chosen, can be a useful supplement, it should not be used exclusively as the primary source for your Bible reading. To explain further, a paraphrase is based on a translation of the Scripture, but it is put into the vernacular of the day, making it easier to read, giving the sense or gist of the passage.

Sometimes the purpose of the user-friendly version is to reach new Christians and younger people. This may involve leaving out elements or adding others with the goal of clarity. But, of course, such an approach is more susceptible to taking on the perspective of the paraphraser, and in some cases, may even have a particular agenda that proves unfaithful to biblical teaching. Through the years there have been many, many paraphrases, some now outdated because of dated expressions. A translation, on the other hand, tries to stay as close as possible to the original text and is usually a phrase-for-phrase rendering of the text from one language to another. The result is truer to the original and more reliable for in-depth Bible study. Reading a reputable translation of the Bible must always be a top priority for a Christian.

—R. d.

190. In 2 Kings 13:14–19, why did King Jehoash mention "the chariots and horsemen of Israel" to the dying Elisha?

Scripture tells us in verse 14 that Elisha, the man of God, is dying of a terminal illness. During his life, Elisha's prophetic ministry was so powerful that even in his dying hour he received a visit from King Jehoash. The king wept before the dying prophet and described to the man of God "the chariots and horsemen of Israel." This important phrase echoes 2 Kings 2:11–12. When the prophet Elijah was swept into Heaven on a chariot and horses made of fire, Elisha used this same phrase in response to witnessing that event.

Chariots and their horsemen were the most powerful military means of waging war and providing national protection in the ancient Near East. In applying "chariot and horsemen" imagery to the dying prophet, Jehoash recognized that the prophet Elisha served as the means of the Lord's moral and spiritual protection of Israel. Jehoash had been a wicked king (see 2 Kings 13:11), but he recognized that Elisha's death would be a great loss to the northern kingdom of Israel. May God raise up some Spirit-empowered Christians to serve as twenty-first-century moral and spiritual *chariots and horsemen and horsewomen* in our own needy day!

—W. N.

191. When Christian teachers disagree, how do I know which one is right? I am talking about arguments over Bible doctrine.

The notion that only one can be right and the other mistaken is not true. In debates about theological issues, sometimes the questions are framed so broadly that both debaters may be right; they approach the question from different angles. They bring out different aspects of truth. So, you have to find out what the respective opponents are trying to prove.

A second consideration is that some theological issues are not worth the energy spent in argument. Take the question said to have been debated in medieval times: how many angels can dance on the head of a pin? The correct answer is, who cares? In other words, arguments about trivial points of doctrine are a waste of time.

How about doctrinal matters such as the timing of Christ's return, whether it is premillennial or postmillennial or somewhere in-between? Which position is correct? That is not a trivial question. It is a serious question about an important doctrine. Some arguments trivialize it, however. Even if we decide a particular position is correct, we need not defend it to the point of alienating fellow believers who disagree.

This attitude of charity relates to "negotiable" questions, matters where honest, godly students of Scripture may disagree. Paul touches on this in Philippians 3:14–15.

Many questions, especially those about the person of Christ, are not negotiable. In trying to answer, "Who is Christ?" there is no wiggle room.

The fact that equally credible Bible students hold opposing positions on serious Bible questions should teach us the folly of dogmatism. As creatures, we are not capable of being perfect in either action or belief. Those who trust in Christ for forgiveness of sins will learn the fullness of perfect truth when we live for eternity with our Creator.

—D. C.

192. I've always been taught that Deborah was chosen to lead as a judge in Israel because no men were willing to do the job. But I see no evidence of that in Scripture. From what I read, she was a judge because she had the people's respect, and they came to her to be judged. Is this accurate?

The story of Deborah is often taught as though God had a Plan A that didn't work out, and Deborah was the back-up choice when Barak defaulted. As you note, however, in Judges 4 and 5, Deborah was already leading Israel when the passage opens (4:4) and is respected as "she held court under the Palm of Deborah" (4:5). Barak doesn't come into the picture until Deborah is established as a leader and a prophetess. In Judges 4:6, Deborah summons Barak and speaks God's word to him before we know what he is going to do.

You're correct—this story has nothing to do with a man not being available. When Barak hears Deborah's message that he is commanded to go to war, he won't do it unless she goes with him (4:8). Deborah then tells Barak the consequences of his refusal. The honor will not be his (4:9) but will go to another woman, Jael, who kills Sisera by hammering a peg into his temple (4:21), a startlingly courageous act.

When one looks at the theme of Judges, consistently people disobey; they often do the wrong thing or only grudgingly do the right thing. We see this in Barak, who doesn't initially trust God. To describe Deborah's judgeship in Israel as the result of no men being willing to do the job is both incorrect and irrelevant. It also diminishes the truth of God's view of women.

Everywhere in Scripture God shows how much He loves, defends, and values women.

—*R. d.*

193. What is meant by the phrase "the poor in spirit" in the Beatitudes?

The Beatitudes speak of the "Happy Ones," those who are blessed because they don't think of themselves more highly than they should (see Matt. 5:3).

The poor in spirit are not spiritually conceited. I'm often concerned about those who get caught up in their own gifts and importance and become almost arrogant before others. Whether we're on the cleanup committee or the speaker before an applauding congregation, we can become so caught up in ourselves that we rarely appreciate the gifts of others or give them the acknowledgment and honor they deserve. We can be so impressed with how far we've come in our earthly or divine gifts or abilities that we forget that any gift or ability comes from Christ, and without Him or His power we would be nothing. But we're admonished to "not think of yourself more highly than you ought" (Rom. 12:3). The Lord is pleased with a right attitude toward Him and others, as James says in 4:10: "Humble yourselves before the Lord, and he will lift you up."

The humble lean on God. The humble man or woman is well aware that their accomplishments are for the glory of God. The humble live with the indwelling principle of Paul: "I have been crucified with Christ and I no longer live, but Christ lives in me" (Gal. 2:20).

—*M. K.*

194. I have friends who I believe are born again, and what often comes up is their very strong belief in purgatory. What does the Bible say about that?

Frankly, I believe that it says absolutely nothing. Purgatory refers to an in-between state where believers go if they die with sins that have not been atoned for before moving on to Heaven. Some suggest that 1 Corinthians 3:13 refers to purgatory, but in fact this verse in context is talking about rewards in Heaven and not salvation.

The problem with the concept of purgatory is that it implies that what Christ Jesus did on Calvary wasn't good enough, and that somehow there will be a further time after death when we can work some more on overcoming sin. This notion implies that Jesus' sacrifice for the believer isn't sufficient, that continued work must be done to make up for sins and earn salvation.

But as the old hymn says, "Jesus paid it all / all to Him I owe." From the cross He underlined the all-sufficiency of Calvary when He said, "It is finished" (John 19:30). We can do nothing to make ourselves fit for Heaven, not through our good works while we are alive on this earth nor through some notion of suffering in purgatory after death. Jesus took the penalty for our sin, and all those who trust in Him now find that "to be away from the body [is to be] at home with the Lord" (2 Cor. 5:8).

—*M. K.*

195. Where did Cain get his wife?

After Cain murdered his brother, Abel, the Lord disciplined him by making him "a restless wanderer on the earth" (Gen. 4:12). Nevertheless, God showed Cain grace in the midst of judgment by placing "a mark on Cain so that no one who found him would kill him" (Gen. 4:15). Cain then settled "in the land of Nod, east of Eden," married, and had a son (Gen. 4:16–17).

If Cain was one of only three sons born to Adam and Eve, where did Cain find this wife? And a related question is who else existed who would potentially want to kill him?

The answer lies in the nature of biblical storytelling, called narrative. One characteristic of the narrative of Scripture is that it is intentionally selective in the information it transmits. Biblical narrative tells only what needs to be known for the story. In the account of Cain and Abel, it was unnecessary to include a description of any other siblings. That does not mean, however, that Adam and Eve did not have other children, both male and female. Indeed, God's command, "Be fruitful and increase in number; fill the earth and subdue it," means it is likely that Adam and Eve had many more children than just the three whose names we are given (Gen. 1:28).

This explains both questions. First, Cain likely feared that his brothers (and possibly also nephews) would want to kill him to avenge the murder of their brother Abel. Thus, God marked Cain to protect him. Second, Cain found a female descendant of Adam and Eve to marry. We don't know how much time had elapsed since the eviction from the garden of Eden or how many descendants of Adam and Eve now filled the world, but it seems like a clear conclusion from this text that the population was sufficient to provide Cain both an option to marry and a reason to fear.

—*M. R.*

196. Was the star the Wise Men followed when they were looking for Jesus visible in the daytime? Or could they see it only at night?

Matthew is our only reliable source of information about the star, and he doesn't give technical details, except to say that the Wise Men first saw the star "when it rose," or as rendered in some versions, "in the east." When the Wise Men left Herod on their way to Bethlehem, "the star that they had seen when it rose went ahead of them until it stopped over the place where the child was. When they saw the star, they were overjoyed" (Matt. 2:2, 9–10).

A legitimate inference from the second statement is that the star that led them from the distant east was invisible as long as they were in Jerusalem, but it reappeared as soon as they set out for Bethlehem. We don't know the time of their departure from Jerusalem. It could have been right after lunch, or after sundown when stars come out. In any case, we do not know for certain whether it was constantly visible to the Wise Men in the daytime.

—*D. C.*

197. Is the "newly discovered" book of Judas a part of the biblical canon?

This is a very serious question. In the early church these kinds of questions were literally life and death matters. Back then it was a real possibility for a Christian to be put to death for protecting and hiding Scripture. Knowing this, godly believers wanted to know which books they should be prepared to die for. They wanted to know which books are divinely inspired, which books are canonical, that is, the authoritative and final standard for faith and practice. Complicating matters was the fact that from the second to the ninth century, various so-called gospels and letters were in circulation with advocates claiming that they were authoritative. In this life-or-death context, the most important criterion for the recognition of what was canonical was apostolicity. Apostolicity means that the book in question was written by one of the apostles or by one of his close associates. Apostolicity also places the date of writing in the first century.

Another criterion for canonical status was the edifying impact of the writing on the individual and collective life of the Christian community. The Gospel of Judas does not meet these criteria. The fact that the Gospel of Judas was probably written in the middle of the second century rules out apostolic authorship. The book certainly is not edifying. In this regard there is almost infinite chasm between the edifying books of the New Testament and the Gospel of Judas. Space does not permit an in-depth discussion of the erroneous and heretical contents of this account. At any rate, the early church rejected the book and considered it to be heretical—and rightly so! The Gospel of

Judas is not a part of the divinely inspired biblical canon.

Let us remember that with their lives often on the line, in time the church understood that the canon of Scripture was closed with the penning of the last book of the Bible, the Revelation of Jesus Christ. But I do ask myself: do we today have the same attitude toward the Bible that the early church did? If it were a real possibility for you to lose your life for having Scripture in your possession, would you be willing to put your life on the line for owning a Bible?

—*W. N.*

198. What does the word "behold" mean?

The Hebrew word *hinneh*, which is translated as "behold" or "look" in English, serves several important functions in Old Testament Scripture. First, it highlights for the reader the significance of the content that follows it. The biblical writer's use of *behold* signals that what a biblical character in a historical narrative sees or experiences immediately after *behold* is very important (see Gen. 22:13; Ex. 3:2). Second, the biblical writer's use of *behold* also alerts readers that the upcoming narrative is very important (1 Sam. 4:3; Prov. 1:23).

Due to the influence of Hebrew idioms on the New Testament writers, we see *behold* (the Greek word *idou*) in the New Testament. The main function is the same. For example, when God's purpose of grace is consummated and He makes His dwelling among redeemed and glorified humanity, John wants to signal to us the wonder and utter importance of this event. Indeed, a voice from Heaven prefaces the occurrence of this great reality with "Behold" or "Look!" (Rev. 21:3–4). To learn more about the use of this word, a concordance is a valuable tool. You could start by looking up the statements and events prefaced with *behold* in the book of Revelation.

—*W. N.*

199. How do we see God's providence in the book of Esther? Does this story have anything to do with our lives today?

Providence is evident throughout the book of Esther in the events that initially appear to be coincidences. Esther just happens to find favor with the royal official in charge of the beauty contest (2:8–9). Mordecai just happens to overhear the plot against the king (2:21–23). The notoriously fickle King Xerxes just happens to point his scepter at Esther in welcome (5:1–3). The king just happens to have insomnia, and the selected reading just happens to be the account of Mordecai saving his life (6:1–2). Haman, the genocidal maniac and hater of Jews, just happens to perish on the same day that he planned the genocide of the Jewish people and on the same gallows that he prepared for Mordecai (7:9–10). As the so-called coincidences pile up, it becomes ever clearer to the reader that actually God's hand is moving and working through these events to save His people.

What does this have to do with us today? The book of Esther has several important lessons that apply to our lives. First, we see that God was active in preserving the Jewish people so the Messiah Jesus could come as the son of David, the son of Abraham (see Matt. 1:1). God would not allow Haman's wicked scheme to succeed, for He had promised to send the Messiah through the line of David. This Messiah Jesus provides the way of salvation and a right relationship with God for each of us who believes in His name.

Second, the book of Esther offers us proof that God is active in the lives of all believers, caring for us, accomplishing His purposes, and protecting us. Even when we fail to be faithful, God is still working in our lives (in ways that we might describe as "behind the scenes") out of His great love and faithfulness to His promises (see Rom. 8:28). Third, the book of Esther reminds us that God is faithful to preserve and protect the Jewish people today and always, a great comfort in this time of growing anti-Semitism. Despite the slaughter planned by Haman and all those who have followed in his footsteps, God will still prevail to save His people.

—*M. R.*

200. Is the Bible the only rule of faith and practice for the child of God?

As 2 Timothy 3:16 says, "All Scripture is God-breathed and is useful for teaching, rebuking, correcting and training in righteousness." Further, all Scripture should point our attention toward our Lord and Savior Jesus Christ. He Himself illustrated this truth on the road to Emmaus: "And beginning with Moses and all the Prophets, he explained to them what was said in all the Scriptures concerning himself" (Luke 24:27). The Bible is inspired by God Himself, and we can add nothing to it that would be equally authoritative (see Rev. 22:18–19).

—*M. K.*

Meet the Writers

Don Cole was the host of Moody Radio's *Open Line* and the first writer of *Today in the Word's* Q and A column. After serving in the South Pacific during World War II, Don returned home and married Naomi. They served as missionaries to Angola for twenty years and returned many times in relief missions. Cole joined the Moody staff in 1971 and became known as Moody's radio pastor. He counseled students and staff behind the scenes, answering their questions about life and the Bible. After retiring in 2008, he was inducted into the National Religious Broadcaster's Hall of Fame. He died in 2014 at age 89.

Rosalie de Rosset is professor of English, homiletics, and literature at Moody Bible Institute, where she has taught since 1969. She has written dozens of articles as well as *Unseduced and Unshaken: The Place of Dignity in a Young Woman's Choices* (Moody Publishers). She earned an MDiv from Trinity Evangelical Divinity School and a PhD from University of Illinois at Chicago.

Mike Kellogg was the longtime host of Moody Radio's *Music Thru the Night*, where late-night listeners appreciated his relaxed yet direct testimony of the Christian life. Before his 2014 retirement, Mike also produced Moody Radio dramas, narrated the New Living Translation of the Bible, and wrote many columns for *Today in the Word*. In 2015 he was inducted into the National Religious Broadcaster's Hall of Fame. A graduate of Cedarville College, Mike and his wife, Nancy, have six children and ten grandchildren.

Winfred O. Neely is professor of biblical exposition and program head of the biblical preaching major at Moody Bible Institute. He and his wife, Stephne, served as missionaries to Senegal, West Africa, before returning to Chicago, where he now ministers as senior pastor of Judson Baptist Church. He earned a DMin from Trinity Evangelical Divinity School and is currently working on a PhD in Old Testament. Dr. Neely has written *How to Overcome Worry* (Moody Publishers) and contributed to *The Moody Handbook of Preaching*, *The Moody Bible Commentary*, and *A Heart for the Community*. He and Stephne have been married for over forty years are the proud parents of four children and grandparents of nine grandchildren.

Eric C. Redmond serves as an assistant professor of Bible at Moody Bible Institute and associate pastor of adult ministries at Calvary Memorial Church in Oak Park, Illinois. In addition to writing for *Today in the Word*, he recently released *Where Are All the Brothers? Straight Answers to Men's Questions about the Church*. Eric earned a ThM from Dallas Theological Seminary and is a PhD candidate at Capital Seminary. He and his wife, Pam, have five children.

David Tae-Kyung Rim teaches philosophy and apologetics at Moody Bible Institute. He encourages students to think well and studies the doctrine of the Trinity to further understand its implications for theology and spirituality. David received his PhD from Trinity Evangelical Divinity School and a ThM from Dallas Theological Seminary. David and his wife, Maria, have twin daughters.

Julie Roys has written for *WORLD* magazine, *The Christian Post*, *Christianity Today*, *Religion News Service*, and *The Federalist*, and is the author of *Redeeming the Feminine Soul: God's Surprising Vision for Womanhood*. Julie earned her master's degree in broadcast journalism from Northwestern University and previously worked as a TV news reporter for a CBS affiliate and as a news writer for WGN-TV and Fox News in Chicago. Julie and her husband, Neal, live in the Chicago suburbs and have three children.

Michael Rydelnik is Professor of Jewish Studies and Bible at Moody Bible Institute and the Host/Bible teacher on *Open Line with Dr. Michael Rydelnik*, answering listener Bible questions every Saturday morning for 235 stations across Moody Radio. The son of Holocaust survivors, he was raised in an observant Jewish home in Brooklyn, New York. Michael trusted in Jesus the Messiah in high school and began teaching the Bible almost immediately. He is the co-editor of and a contributor to *The Moody Bible Commentary*, the author of several other books and a contributor to various books, journals, and study Bibles. Michael and his wife, Eva, have two adult sons who call and write all the time.

Subject Index

The references below correlate to the question numbers

Scripture Index

The references below correlate to the question numbers

TODAY IN THE WORD™

Your Daily Dose of Spiritual Encouragement

Get six months free—daily Bible readings, personal applications, and helpful illustrations.

Start Today
todayintheword.com/angels

What's the law got to do with it?

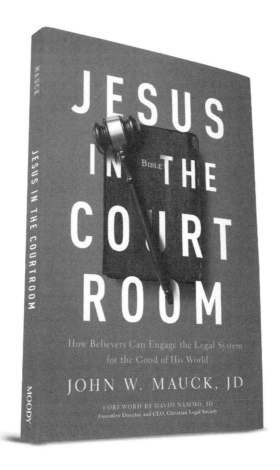

MOODY Publishers

*From the Word **to** Life*

We are citizens of two kingdoms, but many of us duck and run when it comes to civil life. For anyone who cares about their community—parents, teachers, pastors, anyone—*Jesus in the Courtroom* will help you engage with the law for the good of your community and the growth of the gospel.

978-0-8024-1515-8 | ALSO AVAILABLE AS AN EBOOK

Can a Christian ever finish contemplating the Trinity?

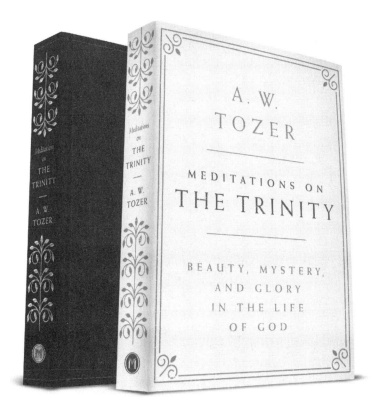

Meditations on the Trinity is a compilation of excerpts from A. W. Tozer, arranged for daily reading. It consists of four parts: one part on each respective person of the Trinity, and one on God three-in-one. Together it offers a more accurate view of who God is, aiding readers in truer worship.

978-1-60066-803-6 | ALSO AVAILABLE AS AN EBOOK

Study the Bible with professors from Moody Bible Institute

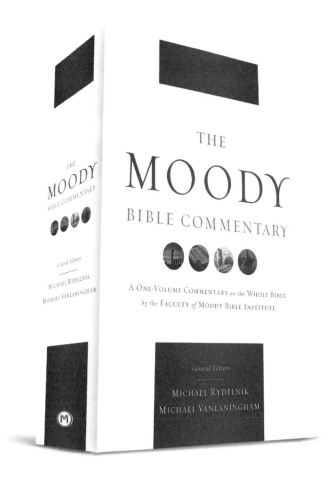

MOODY Publishers®

From the Word to Life®

Study the Bible with a team of 30 Moody Bible Institute professors. This in-depth, user-friendly, one-volume commentary will help you better understand and apply God's written revelation to all of life. Additional study helps include maps, charts, bibliographies for further reading, and a subject and Scripture index.

978-0-8024-2867-7 | ALSO AVAILABLE AS AN EBOOK